FINDING PEACE
through HUMILITY

A BIBLE STUDY IN THE BOOK OF JUDGES

BIBLE STUDY GUIDE | SIX SESSIONS

JOEL MUDDAMALLE

WITH REBECCA ENGLISH LAWSON

HarperChristian
Resources

Finding Peace Through Humility Bible Study Guide
© 2024 Joel Muddamalle

Published in Grand Rapids, Michigan, by HarperChristian Resources. HarperChristian Resources is a registered trademark of HarperCollins Christian Publishing, Inc.

Requests for information should be sent to customercare@harpercollins.com.

ISBN: 978-0-310-16321-3 (softcover)
ISBN: 978-0-310-16322-0 (ebook)

HarperChristian Resources titles may be purchased in bulk for church, business, fundraising, or ministry use. For information, please email ResourceSpecialist@ChurchSource.com.

First printing January 2024 / Printed in the United States of America

CONTENTS

A NOTE FROM JOEL

I hate being lost and losing my way. It leaves me disoriented, and honestly, it can be a really scary feeling to not know where you are. Today, we have modern tools like smartphones that give us maps and directions at our fingertips. But before that technology was available, one of the most vital tools that people used to keep from getting lost was a compass.

A compass shows us which direction we should go and keeps us from going where we should not. God's Word is a type of compass. It points us to where Jesus is and reveals when we start to falter, or get distracted, or are going in a direction that will take us away from him. Yet a compass is only good if we use it. If we fail to keep our focus on it, we will lose our way.

In the book of Judges, we discover this happening to the Israelites. In the days of Moses and Joshua, the people kept their focus on God—their "compass"—and experienced peace. They lived in safety, security, and stability . . . constantly being reminded that the God who had saved them from Egypt would protect them now. This was a peace that came from humility.

But then the Israelites lost their focus on God. They did evil in his sight and worshiped the pagan gods of the peoples around them. This angered the Lord, and "he sold them to the enemies around them, and they could no longer resist their enemies" (Judges 2:14). When the people of Israel lost their humility, they also lost their peace.

The author of Judges frequently reminded his readers that the events of his book took place when "there was no king in Israel" and "everyone did whatever seemed right to him" (Judges 17:6). I want this statement to be an anchor in our minds as we work through this study. Things fell into this state of affairs because the

Israelites had rejected their sovereign King, the Lord God, and chose to do what they thought right in their own eyes.

Before Joshua died, he had challenged the Israelites: "If it doesn't please you to worship the LORD, choose for yourselves today: Which will you worship—the gods your ancestors worshiped beyond the Euphrates River or the gods of the Amorites in whose land you are living? As for me and my family, we will worship the LORD" (Joshua 24:15). We read that at that time, the people promised to follow the Lord. But ultimately, they failed to keep their word.

The question Joshua asked the Israelites is the same question God is asking us today: "Where will your allegiance be? Will it be to counterfeit helpers that provide no help at all? Or will you bend your knee in humility to me, the King of the cosmos, who created you?" Jesus is the King of heaven and earth, the Creator of the cosmos. When we reject him, we are exhibiting pride. But when we recognize our need of a King and focus on him, we are rooted in humility.

Humility . . . that's what we're going to unpack in this study. Humility may not be what we expected, but it's what we need to experience the peace we all long for.

— JOEL MUDDAMALLE, PhD

HOW TO USE THIS GUIDE

When the Israelites lost their focus on God and began serving the false gods of other nations, they fell into a cycle of sin, judgment, remorse, and deliverance. This cycle was like a spiral hurtling them down into utter destruction and defeat, with God sending judges again and again to bail the people out, only for them to fall into sin again. This tragedy didn't have to happen.

Something is hiding in plain sight throughout the pages of Judges: God's desire for his people to pursue and live out humility. A constant posture of humility would have helped them break the cycle of sin and remind them to turn to God, who is the source of lasting peace.

In this Bible study, we will see that the same is true for us. God wants us to be free of the trouble and chaos that is caused by our sin and pride. We find that peace when we choose the path of humility. When we lose our focus on our King, we spiral into the same cycle of chaos the Israelites experienced when they turned to foreign gods. But if we keep our focus on Jesus, realizing that his life alone will sustain and guide us, we will walk in his peace.

Before you begin this study, keep in mind there are a few ways you can go through this material. You can experience the study with others in a small group (such as a Bible study, Sunday school class, or home group), or you may choose to go through the content on your own. Either way, the videos for each session are available for you to view at any time by following the instructions provided with this study guide.

GROUP STUDY

Each session is divided into two parts: (1) a group study section and (2) a personal study section. The group study section provides a basic framework on how to open your time together, get the most out of the video content, and discuss the key ideas together that were presented in the teaching. Each session includes the following:

- **Welcome:** A short note about the topic of the session for you to read on your own before you meet as a group.

- **Connect:** A few icebreaker questions to get you and your group members thinking about the topic and interacting with each other.

- **Watch:** An outline of the key points covered in each video teaching to help you follow along, stay engaged, and take notes.

- **Discuss:** Questions to help your group reflect on the teaching material presented and apply it to your lives.

- **Respond:** A short personal exercise to help reinforce the key ideas.

- **Pray:** A place for you to record prayer requests and praises for the week.

If you are doing this study in a group, make sure you have your own copy of this study guide so you can write down your thoughts, responses, and reflections and have access to the videos via streaming. You will also want to have a copy of *The Hidden Peace*, as reading it alongside the curriculum will provide you with deeper insights. (See the notes at the beginning of each group session and personal study section on which chapters of the book you should read before the next group session.) Finally, keep these points in mind:

- **Facilitation:** If you are doing this study in a group, you will want to appoint someone to serve as a facilitator. This person will be responsible for starting the video and keeping track of time during discussions and activities. If *you* have been chosen for this role, there are some resources in the back of this guide that can help you lead your group through the study.

- **Faithfulness:** Your group is a place where tremendous growth can happen as you reflect on the Bible, ask questions, and learn what God is doing in other people's lives. For this reason, be fully committed and attend each session so you can build trust and rapport with the other members.

- **Friendship:** The goal of any small group is to serve as a place where people can share, learn about God, and build friendships. So seek to make your group a safe place. Be honest about your thoughts and feelings, but also listen carefully to everyone else's thoughts, feelings, and opinions. Keep anything personal that your group members share in confidence so that you can create a community where people can heal, be challenged, and grow spiritually.

If you are going through this study on your own, read the opening Welcome section and reflect on the questions in the Connect section. Watch the video and use the prompts provided to take notes. Finally, personalize the questions and exercises in the Discuss and Respond sections. Close by recording any requests you want to pray about during the week.

PERSONAL STUDY

The personal study is for you to work through on your own during the week. Each exercise is designed to help you explore the key ideas you uncovered during your group time and delve into passages of Scripture that will help you apply those principles to your life. Go at your own pace, doing a little each day—or tackle the material all at once. Remember to spend a few moments in silence to listen to whatever the Holy Spirit might be saying to you.

Each section contains three personal studies that open with a brief devotion for you to read, a few passages for you to look up, and several reflection questions to help you apply the truths of God's Word to your life. Following this, there is a Connect & Discuss page with several questions for you to answer with a friend, either over a phone call or a cup of coffee. Finally, the Catch Up & Read Ahead page will give you a chance to finish any uncompleted personal studies and read the upcoming chapters in *The Hidden Peace*.

Note that if you are doing this study as part of a group and are unable to finish (or even start) these personal studies for the week, you should still attend the group time. Be assured that you are wanted and welcome even if you don't have your "homework" done. The group and personal studies are intended to help you hear what God wants you to hear and learn how to apply it to your life. So as you go through this study, be listening for what God has to say to you about how humility brings peace. Whether you walk through good times or bad, when you focus on Jesus, you will experience the peace of God that will guard your heart and mind.

When arrogance comes, disgrace follows,
but with humility comes wisdom.

PROVERBS 11:2

ISRAEL UNDER THE JUDGES

Mediterranean Sea

SHAMGAR?

Hazor (Jabin)

Acco

ELON

Sea of Galilee

Kishon R.

Kedesh
(Barak)

Harosheth
(Sisera)

▲ *Mt. Tabor*

JAIR

Kamon

Megiddo

GIDEON

Ophrah

Jabesh
Gilead

Abel
Meholah

TOLA

Shamir

Jordan R.

Jabbok R.

Pirathon

▲ *Mt. Ebal*
▲ *Mt. Gerizim*

ABDON

Mizpah

Shiloh

JEPHTHAH

Gilead

Bethel

DEBORAH

Rabbah

EHUD

Ramah

Jericho
(City of Palms)

Timnah

AMMONITES

Ashdod

Zorah

Eshtaol

Jerusalem

Bethlehem

Ashkelon

SAMSON

IBZAN

*Tableland
of Moab
(Mishor)*

PHILISTINES

Gaza

Hebron

*Dead
Sea*

OTHNIEL

Debir

Arnon Gorge

Othniel	Judges 3:7–11
Ehud	Judges 3:12–30
Shamgar	Judges 3:31
Deborah	Judges 4–5
Gideon	Judges 6–8
Tola	Judges 10:1–2
Jair	Judges 10:3–5
Jephthah	Judges 10:6–12:7
Ibzan	Judges 12:8–10
Elon	Judges 12:11–12
Abdon	Judges 12:13–15
Samson	Judges 13–16

Beersheba

MOABITES

EDOMITES

0   10 km.
0   10 miles

WEEK 1

BEFORE GROUP MEETING	Read chapters 1–2 in *The Hidden Peace* Read the Welcome section (page 2)
GROUP MEETING	Discuss the Connect questions Watch the video teaching for session 1 Discuss the questions that follow as a group Do the closing exercise and pray (pages 2–6)
STUDY 1	Complete the personal study (pages 9–11)
STUDY 2	Complete the personal study (pages 12–14)
STUDY 3	Complete the personal study (pages 15–17)
CONNECT & DISCUSS	Connect with someone in your group (page 18)
CATCH UP & READ AHEAD (BEFORE WEEK 2 GROUP MEETING)	Read chapters 3–5 in *The Hidden Peace* Complete any unfinished personal studies (page 19)

STUCK IN THE CYCLE

*In those days there was no king in Israel;
everyone did whatever seemed right to him.*

JUDGES 17:6

WELCOME | READ ON YOUR OWN

None of us likes to have chaos in our lives. We don't want to experience the tension, anxiety, fear, and all the other unpleasant emotions and realities that chaos can bring. We would rather enjoy peace.

The people of Israel desired peace . . . and God had promised they could have it if they followed his commands. But instead, during the time of the judges, the people often fell away from God and slipped into idolatry. As a result, God would send judgment against them in the form of an enemy nation to harass and oppress them. The Israelites, reeling from their pain, would remember the Lord and cry out to him, and God would faithfully send judges to lead them out of trouble and back to himself, where they could find peace. This happened again and again.

Why did the Israelites constantly fall out of peace and back into chaos? Because they kept rejecting the Lord God—their one and only King. They wanted to be like the peoples around them, and they wanted the perceived security of the other nations' gods. So they allowed things like fear, ambition, and pain to drive their decisions. But at the bottom of all this was *pride*. God had told them how to live and provided them with his guidance. Yet they drifted away from him because they thought they knew better.

God wants us to live in peace—and we do this through humility. When we realize that we need a King and surrender ourselves to him, he will fill us with his rest.

CONNECT | 15 MINUTES

If any of your group members don't know each other, take a few minutes to introduce yourselves. Then, to get things started, discuss one of the following questions:

- What is your primary goal or hope for participating in this study? (In other words, why are you here?)

  — *or* —

- What is one thing that causes you to lose your sense of peace?

WATCH | 20 MINUTES

Now watch the video for this session, which you can access by playing the DVD or through streaming (see the instructions provided with this study guide). As you watch, use the following outline to record any thoughts or concepts that stand out to you.

OUTLINE

I. God's Word is a compass for our lives that always points us toward Jesus.
   A. Humility enables us to be led by the Scriptures and makes us aware when we get distracted and start to go to places that we should not go.
   B. God served as a compass for the Israelites. He led them out of Egypt and made his presence known through a pillar of fire by night and pillar of cloud by day.
   C. God led them safely through the Red Sea—an image of chaos—and closed the waters on the pursuing Egyptians. He eventually led them into the promised land.

II. The Israelites, in the promised land, lost their focus on God after Joshua's death.
   A. The people's awareness of God was the framework that established humility in their lives. As long as they kept their focus on the Lord, they experienced his peace.
   B. Humility is what flows out of us when we see God as he truly is and see ourselves in light of who God is—which then helps us to see others as God does.
   C. The Israelites exchanged their focus, attention, and affection for God with the false gods of the Canaanites. When this happened, they lost their peace.

III. We need to connect the dots on who these gods were and what they represented.
   A. Baal was the god of thunder and lightning who provided water and rain for crops. The temptation for the Israelites was to pray to him to secure a successful harvest.
   B. Ishtar was the war goddess. The temptation for the Israelites was to pray to her for success in battle if the odds seemed to not be stacked in their favor.
   C. Dagon was a fish deity and Ashtoreth was a fertility goddess. The temptation for the Israelites was to pray to these deities for food and for offspring.
   D. Counterfeit gods are still present today. They just wear different masks, like social media, money, resources, family, vocation, education, and accomplishments.

IV. Judges frequently states that there was no king in Israel (see 17:6; 18:1; 19:1; 21:25).
   A. Joshua gave the people a choice: God or idols. The people ultimately chose idols.
   B. The cycle of the Israelites' sin: (1) they turned from God; (2) God responded with judgment; (3) they cried out for mercy; (4) God delivered them through judges.
   C. A constant posture of humility would have enabled the Israelites to break free of this cycle of sin and would have reminded them to turn their focus back to God.

NOTES

_____

_____

_____

_____

_____

_____

_____

_____

_____

_____

_____

_____

_____

_____

_____

_____

_____

_____

_____

_____

_____

_____

_____

_____

_____

_____

_____

_____

_____

_____

_____

_____

_____

_____

_____

DISCUSS | 35 MINUTES

Now discuss what you just watched by answering the following questions.

1. A compass guides us, and if we look to it, it can lead us to our destination. But if we lose focus on it, or focus on the wrong part of it, things will spiral out of control. How was this true in the Israelites' case after the death of Joshua?

2. God had miraculously delivered his people out of Egypt, led them in a pillar of cloud by day and a pillar of fire by night, and made a way for them to safely pass through the Red Sea. Yet even though God had guided the Israelites so miraculously, the people gradually forgot him. How does such a loss of focus on God and a loss of humility go hand in hand?

3. Consider this definition of *humility* from this week's teaching: "Humility is what flows out of us when we see God as he truly is and see ourselves in light of who God is—which then helps us to see others as God does." How does seeing God accurately enable you to see yourself more honestly? How does this affect your relationships with others?

4. When the Israelites lost their focus on God, they actually *exchanged* their focus on him for something else that was false. What were some of the false gods the Israelites chose to serve—and why? What are some counterfeit gods that people serve today?

5. "In those days there was no king in Israel; everyone did whatever seemed right to him" (Judges 17:6). What did the author of Judges mean by making this statement? How would humility and reverence toward God have broken the Israelites out of their cycle of sin?

RESPOND | 10 MINUTES

Before his death, Joshua gave a speech in which he reminded the Israelites of God's faithfulness. He then gave them a choice: worship God, or follow idols (see Joshua 24:14–15). Sadly, when we come to the book of Judges, we find that the people ultimately chose idols, which led to a cycle of sin, judgment, remorse, and deliverance. Fortunately, we don't have to end up the same! Take a few minutes on your own to consider what might be tempting *you* to take your focus off God. Use the following questions to help guide you in this reflection.

What one thing most distracts you from keeping your focus on God?

Why do you think that particular issue is tripping you up?

What do you sense God is prompting you to do to address this problem?

PRAY | 10 MINUTES

Praying for one another is one of the most important things you can do as a community. So use this prayer time wisely, and make it more than just a "closing prayer" to end your group experience. Be intentional about sharing your prayer requests, reviewing how God is answering your prayers, and praying for each other as a group. As you pray, ask God to help you walk in humility before him and keep you from the cycle of sin and chaos that the Israelites modeled. Before you close your session, write down any requests so that you and your fellow group members can continue to pray about them in the week ahead.

SESSION ONE

PERSONAL STUDY

As you heard during the group time, God's Word is like a compass that points you "due north" to Jesus. But when you fail to focus on Jesus and instead focus on the things of this world, your heart and mind end up disturbed and unsettled. This week, you will have the opportunity to look at a few verses to see what the Bible says about why the Israelites kept spiraling into chaos and how you can avoid the same fate. As you consider these passages, ask God to reveal what he wants you to learn. He has something specific for you to take away from this study! Be sure to write down your responses as you work through these questions, as you will be given a few minutes to share your insights if you are doing this study with a group. If you are reading *The Hidden Peace* alongside this study, first review chapters 1–2 in the book.

FOLLOW THE LEADER

Imagine the scene: thousands and thousands of people—along with their cattle, carts, and everything they own—are following Moses into the wilderness to escape slavery in Egypt.[1] The Lord has guided them through a desert to the edge of the Red Sea. But now, in a horrifying turn of events, the king of Egypt and his army have been seen approaching the people's location. The Israelites are trapped. They cry out to Moses, "Why did you bring us out here to die?"

Most of us have felt trapped at one time or another in our lives. We have all endured seasons in which it felt like no matter what we did, we couldn't seem to make progress and move ahead. For some of us, these seasons were mercifully short. For others, these seasons stretched on for months and even years. There were times when things looked hopeless.

When we are boxed in, the last thing that we think about is humility. Much like the Israelites at the Red Sea, we tend to panic and blame the people who we think led us into the jam that we are facing. We lose our faith in God and complain that there is no way out.

But think about it for a moment. The Bible is clear that it was *God* who led the Israelites to that impossible place. And God had the answer to their problem—an answer they couldn't see because it was supernatural. But the people had to exercise humility and trust in God. Moses told the people, "The LORD will fight for you, and you must be quiet" (Exodus 14:14). Instead of panicking, they needed to get still and be humble before the Lord.

The Lord has the answer to our problems as well. He can take us out of any situation in which we are feeling stuck. He may not open up a path through the sea like he did for the Israelites, but he will definitely lead us out of chaos and into his peace. But first, we have to still ourselves before God, trust in his provision, and humbly allow him to lead us forward.

READ | Exodus 14:1–31; Psalm 46:1–11; Psalm 77:19–20

REFLECT

1. When is a time in your life that you were trapped by circumstances and felt as if you had no way out?

2. What do you tend to do first when you can't see an answer to your situation> Do you respond in panic? If so, how do the words of Exodus 14:13–14 help you?

> We were created with innate humility in our hearts, so if we lose humility, we actually lose part of God's design for humanity. When we live in a way that is inconsistent with how God designed us to live (humble), there is an incongruity between who we are and who we are meant to be. In other words, we struggle to live out what God intended for us. God created humanity in his image, which gives us intrinsic worth and value.[2]

3. What does it mean that "we were created with innate humility in our hearts"? How does *not* being humble keep you from handling life the way God intends you to handle it?

> The promise of Psalm 46 is the presence of the King in the midst of our fear—the King who personally walks us through our pain. We have a Battle Leader. He will meet us in our panic moments, our living nightmares, and bring his power into the picture. All eleven verses of Psalm 46 can encourage our fearful hearts as they assure us that God is in total control over all things. The psalmist breaks it up into three categories: God is in control over nature (verses 1–3), over our enemies (verses 4–7), and over the entire world that is in war and chaos (verses 8–11).[3]

4. Review each of these three categories of God's control in Psalm 46. In the box below, write down how the psalmist's words about control over those areas provides you with peace.

God is in control over nature (verses 1–3).	
God is in control over those who would seek to do you harm (verses 4–7).	
God is in control over the entire world that is in war and chaos (verses 8–11).	

5. Psalm 77:19–20 says that God's footprints are "unseen." How does it comfort you to know that God already has a way out of your dilemma—even before you see it?

PRAY | End your time in prayer. Thank God that he is a faithful leader, and ask him to help you quietly and humbly trust his guidance.

STUDY 2

DON'T LOSE YOUR FOCUS!

Have you ever been distracted by what you thought was a small temptation, only to find yourself tangled up in a big mess? The Israelites did—again and again.

First, they would succumb to the temptation to turn to false gods like Baal, Ishtar, or Ashtoreth to provide rain, success in battle, and children. This would lead to the people doing evil in God's sight, and the Lord would respond by executing his judgment. This led to the Israelites crying out to God for mercy. The Lord would hear their prayers and send a deliverer in the form of a judge. Sadly, once that judge died, the people would start all over, turning again from God to idols.

It's easy to fall into this cycle. When our focus on Jesus slips and we get distracted, it can turn even good things into god-type things. We prioritize social media, money, career, education, friends, or even family over God—and it becomes idolatry. As we heard in this week's teaching, "Whatever we long for, we will look for, and it will eventually become what we love." Loving other things above Jesus waters down our love for him. When we finally wake up and cry out to the Lord, he helps us—and then we are tempted by the same things again.

How do we keep our focus on God instead of being constantly pulled into the cycle of sin? It is found in humility. Humility makes us aware of our destructive patterns. Humility positions us for rescue from temptation and ensures our peace. If the Israelites had just adopted a constant posture of humility, they would have avoided the cycle of sin. The same is true for us, as James 4:6 makes clear: "God resists the proud but gives grace to the humble."

READ | Judges 2:11–19; James 4:6–10; Proverbs 16:18

REFLECT

1. In the following list, put a check beside any item that tends to draw your focus away from God. In the space that follows, write down how being drawn away from the Lord by one of these things has affected your life.

☐ social media   ☐ money
☐ career   ☐ education
☐ friends   ☐ family

2. Review Judges 2:11–19. What were some of the things the Israelites did to perpetuate the cycle of sin . . . even while God was showing them mercy by giving them judges to help them? How does this reveal an attitude of pride?

I want to invite you to come and see how God alone can grant us the peace we long and hope for. But before we can get into that, we need some honest exploration. . . . To be honest, things may get difficult as we face longings of our hearts that need reorientation. But all of this, I promise you, is good. . . . Typically, in order to get to the good, we need to go through some hard.[4]

3. God is the only one who can give us the peace that we so desire. So why do you think that so many people today look for peace in so many other places?

4. The letter of James is filled with teachings that we might consider to be "hard" in order to get us to God's greater "good" for our lives. What to you is the most reassuring statement found in James 4:6–10? How will it help you keep your focus on Jesus?

One way or another, you and I have tried to take things into our own hands and, in so doing, we've viewed humility as unwanted and unnecessary. Yet amid all our angst and fear and opposition to humility, *it is actually humility that will move us forward*, into the life we're longing for.[5]

5. "Pride comes before destruction, and an arrogant spirit before a fall" (Proverbs 16:18). How does a spirit of humility before God keep us off the path of destruction? How does humility actually move us *forward* into the life that we are longing to receive from God?

PRAY | End your time in prayer. Thank God for his willingness to rescue you from the cycle of sin. Ask him to give you a continual posture of humility.

THE UNEXPECTED ANSWER

As noted in this week's teaching, before Joshua died, he challenged the people of Israel to choose God over idols. They replied, "We will certainly not abandon the LORD to worship other gods!" (Joshua 24:16). Sadly, their good intentions failed. After Joshua and the elders who outlived him died, "another generation rose up who did not know the LORD or the works he had done for Israel" (Judges 2:10).

The author of Judges shed some light on this period in Israel's history: "In those days there was no king in Israel; everyone did whatever seemed right to him" (17:6). In addition to stating that Israel had no physical king at this time, the verse also implies that Israel had rejected God as king. The people refused to humble themselves before God and instead exalted themselves, which, as we will see throughout Judges, led to continual sin and judgment.

Humility was the unexpected answer to the people's troubles. While the word *humility* doesn't show up in the pages of the book, it is hiding all over the text in plain sight. If the people of Israel had only humbled themselves before God, they would have avoided the cycle of sin and enjoyed the peace God intended them to have.

The church father Augustine once wrote the following to a student: "I desire you to submit yourself with unreserved piety, and I wish you to prepare for yourself no other way of seizing and holding the truth than that which has been prepared by Him who, as God, saw the weakness of our goings. In that way the first part is humility; the second, humility; the third, humility: and this I would continue to repeat as often as you might ask direction, not that there are no other instructions which may be given, but because, unless humility precede, accompany, and follow every good action which we perform, being at once the object which we keep before our eyes, the support to which we cling, and the monitor by which we are restrained, pride wrests wholly from our hand any good work on which we are congratulating ourselves."[6]

Humility may not be what we expect when it comes to dealing with the chaos in our lives. But if we truly want God's peace, it's what we need.

READ | Joshua 24:14–28; Judges 2:7–10; Proverbs 11:2; Romans 12:3–8

REFLECT

1. In Joshua 24:14–28, we see the people had every intention of worshiping the Lord and obeying him alone. When is a time that you likewise promised to love and serve God in some way but failed to follow through on your intentions? As you reflect on that moment, what caused you to fail to follow through?

2. According to Judges 2:7–10, the people faithfully served God throughout Joshua's lifetime. How do you think Joshua was able to keep the people focused on the Lord and away from idols? What did he and the people of that day "know" about God?

3. According to Proverbs 11:2, what does arrogance, or pride, produce? What does humility bring? How have you seen this at work in your own life?

[You may think] humility is a threat that will squash down your strengths and potential. I want to show you that it's actually a gift that helps the best of who we are flourish. You may think it will leave you unstable and weak. I want to show you it will actually make you steady and strong. . . . I need humility because, honestly, I've tried everything else, and none of it has worked.[7]

4. Do you view humility as a threat or a gift? In the boxes below, list some ways that humility might feel like a threat to you and some ways that it could actually be a gift in your life.

Humility as a Threat	Humility as a Gift

> If we think too highly of ourselves, we'll view every relationship through the lens of opportunity. We'll see every person as a pawn on a chessboard for us to move around and even sacrifice for our own benefit. When we receive praise, we will fall into an addictive cycle of desiring it and trying to absorb it until it eventually crushes us. We were never designed to absorb the praise of others; we were designed to pour out praise onto God.[8]

5. What did Paul write in Romans 12:3–8 about the need for humility in the body of Christ? What happens when one "part" gets out of alignment with the rest?

PRAY | End your time in prayer. Ask God to grow in you his gift of humility—through whatever means he chooses. Thank him for the peace it will bring.

CONNECT & DISCUSS

Take time today to connect with a group member and talk about some of the insights from this session. Use any of the prompts below to help guide your discussion.

What is one new thing you learned this week about being humble before God?

How did the challenge not to panic but rather to be quiet before God help you?

What is one change you can make to help you better focus on God and guard against exchanging that focus for something else?

Augustine wrote that humility must "precede, accompany, and follow every good action." What happens when humilty is not at the root of our actions?

In what area would you like to grow as you seek God's peace through humility?

CATCH UP & READ AHEAD

Use this time to go back and complete any of the study and reflection questions from previous days that you weren't able to finish. Make a note below of any questions you've had and reflect on any growth or personal insights you've gained.

Read chapters 3–5 in *The Hidden Peace* before the next group session. Use the space below to make note of anything that stands out to you or encourages you.

WEEK 2

BEFORE GROUP MEETING	Read chapters 3–5 in *The Hidden Peace* Read the Welcome section (page 22)
GROUP MEETING	Discuss the Connect questions Watch the video teaching for session 2 Discuss the questions that follow as a group Do the closing exercise and pray (pages 22–26)
STUDY 1	Complete the personal study (pages 29–31)
STUDY 2	Complete the personal study (pages 32–34)
STUDY 3	Complete the personal study (page 35–37)
CONNECT & DISCUSS	Connect with someone in your group (page 38)
CATCH UP & READ AHEAD (BEFORE WEEK 3 GROUP MEETING)	Read chapters 6–7 in *The Hidden Peace* Complete any unfinished personal studies (page 39)

DON'T LET FEAR LEAD YOU

*Barak said to her, "If you will go with me, I will go.
But if you will not go with me, I will not go."*

JUDGES 4:8

WELCOME | READ ON YOUR OWN

We will encounter a number of hurdles in our journey to find God's peace through humility. One of these hurdles is fear. When we are faced with a threat, God's peace can seem elusive.

In the first session, we discussed how the Israelites fell into a cycle of sin after the death of Joshua. In the first three cycles, God raised up the judges Othniel, Ehud, and Shamgar to deliver the people. In the fourth cycle, God sent a prophet named Deborah to call on a warrior named Barak to be the people's deliverer. Barak was given the task of raising an army to free the Israelites from the forces of King Jabin of Canaan.

Deborah told Barak the Lord had commanded him to go and had promised him victory. Yet Barak hesitated. Why? *Fear.* Ultimately, with Deborah's support, Barak rose to the occasion and delivered Israel from King Jabin's cruelty. Still, his fear cost him the honor of the victory. Deborah prophesized that a *woman* would get the credit for delivering the decisive blow. But the good news is Barak's fear became an opportunity for faith, as he humbled himself and stepped out to obey the Lord. His obedience led to forty years of peace for Israel.

Fear can be debilitating. Thankfully, it can also be an opportunity for us to exercise faith. When we humbly trust God—regardless of the situation we face and how overwhelming it seems—the Lord will give us the strength and peace we need to fulfill his will.

CONNECT | 15 MINUTES

Take a few minutes to get better acquainted with fellow members. Then choose one of the following questions to discuss as a group:

- What is something that spoke to your heart in last week's personal study that you would like to share with the group?

  — *or* —

- What situations in your life cause you the greatest amount of fear?

WATCH | 20 MINUTES

Now watch the video for this session. Below is an outline of the key points covered during the teaching. Record any key concepts that stand out to you.

OUTLINE

I. We all have different responses to fear—we run away from it, face it, or panic.

   A. Some of the major fears that people have:

- *acrophobia*: fear of heights
- *aquaphobia*: fear of water
- *claustrophobia*: fear of closed spaces
- *enochlophobia*: a fear of crowds
- *aerophobia*: fear of flying
- *astraphobia*: fear of storms
- *dentophobia*: fear of the dentist
- *glossophobia*: fear of public speaking

   B. Peace is what we all long to have, but it seems elusive when faced with fear.

II. Israel had fallen back into a cycle of sin and was being oppressed by King Jabin.

   A. The Israelites cried out to God not in *repentance* but for *deliverance*. The source of their request was not made from humble hearts.

   B. God desired that the Israelites would walk in humility. This would have pulled them out of the cycle of sin. God desires the same for each of us today.

   C. When we know who God is and who we are, we are pulled out of cycles of sin that create chaos and experience the peace only the Lord can provide.

III. God called Deborah to go to Barak and challenge him to face King Jabin's army.

   A. Deborah is the only judge identified as actually judging cases. She was also a "prophetess," which means that she served as the mouthpiece of God.

   B. Barak, whose name means "lightning," was called by God to take down Baal, the god of thunder.

   C. Barak was willing to fight Sisera, the Canaanite general, on the condition that Deborah go with him. Barak was guaranteed God's success . . . but he was afraid.

   D. Fear is not an obstacle to exercising faith. Just like Barak, verbalizing and saying we need God in the midst of our fear is a sign of humble strength.

IV. Barak, in spite of his reluctance and fear, is still credited in Scripture as a hero.

   A. Deborah informed Barak that the credit for killing Sisera would go to a woman. We expect this to be Deborah, but that's not the case.

   B. Barak is still credited as a hero (see 1 Samuel 12:11; Hebrews 11:32; Judges 5:12).

   C. Fear placed Barak in a posture of humility. Deborah, in humility, agreed to go with him. Both of them, in humility, gave the final credit to someone else.

   D. We can likewise learn to look at our fears as opportunities to trust in God.

NOTES

DISCUSS | 35 MINUTES

Now discuss what you just watched by answering the following questions.

1. Ask someone to read aloud Judges 4:1–3. The Hebrew word for "cried out" in verse 3 is *tsa'aq*, and it means "to cry out in distress." The Israelites were not repenting when they cried, just asking God for deliverance. Why do you think God chose to help them in spite of this fact? What does this say about his nature and character?

2. Deborah was a judge who judiciously handled civic responsibilities that required her attention but was also a prophetess. What duties did she perform in her role as a prophetess?

3. Barak, whose name means "lightning," was called to fight against those who worshiped Baal, the god of thunder. It would seem he was perfectly positioned to be lightning in God's hands to take down the Canaanites' false god. But how did Barak respond to God's call? What are some of the reasons as to why he might have responded this way?

4. Ask someone to read aloud Judges 5:12, 1 Samuel 12:11, and Hebrews 11:32. Each of these verses describe Barak as a man who faithfully followed God's call to action even though he initially had hesitations. What does this say about the way that God used him in spite of his fears? How does his story encourage you in your faith?

5. Paul wrote, "I will most gladly boast all the more about my weaknesses, so that Christ's power may reside in me" (2 Corinthians 12:9). Acknowledging that you need God in the midst of your fears is a not sign of cowardice but of humble strength. In what area of your life do you need to acknowledge your fears and weaknesses and bring them to God?

RESPOND | 10 MINUTES

We all face many fears in our lives. But when fear comes knocking at our doors, we have a choice as to how we will respond. We can freeze, we can run, we can panic—or we can ask God to provide us with his peace so we can move forward in spite of our fears. How do you tend to respond when you feel afraid? Take a few minutes on your own to consider how you might be allowing fear to lead you. Use the questions below to help guide you in this reflection.

What is one fear right now that is keeping you from experiencing God's peace?

How might this fear be getting in the way of how God wants to use you to serve him?

How do you think humility could help you find peace in this situation?

PRAY | 10 MINUTES

End your time by praying together as a group. As you pray, ask the Lord to help you quiet your heart before him so that he can override your fears with his truth and strength and give you his peace. Ask if anyone has prayer requests, and then write down those requests so that you and your fellow group members can continue to pray about them in the week ahead.

SESSION TWO

PERSONAL STUDY

As you learned in this week's group time, fear can keep you from the peace that God intends you to have. Fear can even keep you from stepping into the role that God has for you. This could have been the case with Barak. But fortunately, he acknowledged his need (in the form of asking Deborah to accompany him) and overcame the Canaanites. This week, you will have the opportunity to look at a few verses to see what the Bible says about fear—and how humility can strengthen your faith and bring about peace. As you work through the exercises, be sure to write down your responses to the questions, as you will be given a few minutes to share your insights at the start of the next session if you are doing this study with others. If you are reading *The Hidden Peace* alongside this study, first review chapters 3–5 in the book.

DON'T MISS YOUR CALLING

In what ways has God called you to serve him? Maybe the Lord has gifted you to serve the poor, be hospitable, teach, work with children, or take the gospel to those who don't know Jesus. Sometimes, though, you will feel afraid to step into God's will.

This was Barak's problem. Before Deborah challenged him to fight the Canaanites, God had already commanded him, "Go, deploy the troops on Mount Tabor, and take with you ten thousand men from the Naphtalites and Zebulunites" (Judges 4:6). Not only that, but God had promised him the victory: "Then I will lure Sisera commander of Jabin's army, his chariots, and his infantry at the Wadi Kishon to fight against you, and I will hand him over to you" (verse 7). With a calling and a promise like that, how could Barak fail?

Still, he hesitated. As we read in the story, "Barak said to [Deborah], 'If you will go with me, I will go. But if you will not go with me, I will not go'" (verse 8). While some believe this suggests cowardice on Barak's part, others believe that he just wanted the security of having God's prophetess by his side. Regardless of the reason, he hesitated but still went.

In times of fear, we can freak out or we can exercise faith. In the New Testament, when Peter and John were arrested and ordered by the religious leaders "not to speak or teach at all in the name of Jesus" (Acts 4:18), they certainly felt fear. But when they were released, they gathered with the other believers and prayed, "Lord, consider their threats, and grant that your servants may speak your word with all boldness" (4:29). Like Barak, they felt fear but exercised faith.

God has placed you exactly where you are at this moment in history to serve him. So step out humbly in obedient faith. As you do, God will fill you with the strength to do his will.

READ | Judges 4:1–8; Acts 17:26–29; Acts 4:1–22

REFLECT

1. Deborah's statement, "Hasn't the LORD . . . commanded you," in Judges 4:6 suggests that at some point in time, the Lord had previously commanded Barak to deploy his troops against King Jabin. Why do you think Barak up to this point had not obeyed that command?

2. How do you feel that God has gifted you or called you to serve him? When have you, like Barak, hesitated to obey God when you sensed that he was leading you?

There is not an ounce of our human life that is random or by chance. Think of it this way: you and I could have lived in any point of human history, yet we live now. There is a purpose to why we live in this specific moment in history. We could be located in any geographical location, yet we live in the country, state, city, neighborhood, street we do for a reason! It's not random. It's not out of control. It is ordered and has a purpose.[9]

3. According to Paul's words to the people of Athens in Acts 17:26–29, God created every person to live in a specific place and time and for a specific purpose. "There is not an ounce of our human life that is random or by chance." How does knowing this give you more confidence to trust in God completely for whatever he is asking you to do?

4. The story of Peter and John in Acts 4:1–22 reveals that we can choose to exercise faith when confronted with fear. What specific fear-inducing situation did Peter and John face? How did the Jewish religious leaders respond to Peter and John's boldness?

> What if our lack of control—even when it leads to anxious nighttime thoughts, moments of panic, and desperate attempts to gain control—is actually a gracious gift of God? What if it sets us up to realize that the very belief that we can control things is really an illusion? As soon as we can identify it as an illusion, we are positioned in a posture of humility and recognize the one who is truly in control of all things. Then, we are straight shook when we look to our side and realize he's been with us the whole time.[10]

5. How do you respond to this idea that a lack of control in your life could actually be a gracious gift from God? How could being "out of control" refocus you on God?

PRAY | End your time in prayer. Ask God to show you what he wants you to do for him and to give you a humble and courageous heart to overcome any fear you have in doing it.

NO CONDITIONS

We sometimes like to put conditions on obeying God's commands. "I will be kind to that coworker when she starts to be nicer to me." "I will study the Bible more faithfully when I'm not quite so busy." "I will start tithing regularly when I make more money and am financially secure." The problem is that the Bible doesn't give us any room for such conditional obedience. As Jesus said to his disciples, "If you love me, you will keep my commands" (John 14:15).

In this week's story, we saw that when Deborah challenged Barak to obey God and fight Sisera, he put conditions on his obedience: "If you will go with me, I will go. But if you will not go with me, I will not go" (Judges 4:8). Deborah informed Barak that his fear and conditional obedience would cause him loss: "You will receive no honor on the road you are about to take, because the LORD will sell Sisera to a woman" (verse 9). At that point, Barak could have changed his tune, but there is no indication that he relented on the conditions he had set.

It would have been so much better if Barak had humbly said, "Yes, I will go. I've been afraid, but I need to trust that God will give me the victory and do what he has asked me to do." Still, to his credit, when Deborah said to him, "Go! This is the day the LORD has handed Sisera over to you" (verse 14), he rallied his forces and charged down from Mount Tabor. And God, *very much* to his credit, rewarded Barak with a victory over Sisera's army.

Barak's story reveals that God will use us for his purposes even when we hold back partially in fear. But why not choose the better course to obey God completely and wholeheartedly? Why not adopt the attitude of the psalmist, who wrote, "Just tell me what to do and I will do it, Lord. As long as I live I'll wholeheartedly obey" (Psalm 119:33–34 TLB)? If God has commanded us to do something, we can rely on the fact that he will provide the means for us to accomplish it. So let's humble ourselves, depend on his grace, and commit to saying, "No conditions, Lord! I may be weak, but I know that in you, I am strong."

READ | Judges 4:8–16; Romans 8:28; Psalm 20:7; Proverbs 3:5–6; 2 Kings 6:15–20

REFLECT

1. What is an example from your own life of putting conditions on God in order to obey an instruction that he gave you? Looking back, how might those conditions you placed on God have affected the outcome of the situation?

2. Paul wrote, "We know that all things work together for the good of those who love God, who are called according to his purpose" (Romans 8:28). Even though Barak allowed his fear to impact his response to God's command, the Lord still rewarded him with a victory. How have you seen God likewise come through for you even when you hesitated in obeying him?

You can simply accept the limits of your weakness and allow that to lead you into further safe dependence on God. Be encouraged that your brave honesty—your willingness to accept the reality of your weakness and who God says you are—will not ultimately diminish you. It will actually produce humility, nudging you to lean more and more into Jesus' power, putting you on the path toward infinite strength.[11]

3. One reason we put conditions on our obedience to God is because we want to assume some level of control. In Barak's case, having Deborah at his side provided him with assurance that God's presence would be with him in the battle. According to Psalm 20:7, in what should Barak have placed his faith instead?

4. What phrases from Proverbs 3:5–6 imply that we should have an attitude of humility as we walk with God? How will God respond when we are humble before him?

The great theologian J. I. Packer wrote, "Weakness is the way."[12] It's the way for us to come to terms with our limits. It reminds us of what we can do and what we can't do. The reality of weakness lets us off the hook of expectations of perfection. In a way, weakness is the prerequisite to God giving us help. As Scripture tells us, "While we were still weak, at the right time Christ died for the ungodly" (Romans 5:6 ESV).[13]

5. Accepting our limitations allows us to recognize that while we might not see a way forward, the Lord will always provide a way. He is working in ways that we simply are not always able to discern. In the story told in 2 Kings 6:15–20, what did Elisha pray for his servant? What did God (through Elisha) reveal to the servant in that situation?

PRAY | End your time in prayer. Ask God to help you obey him without conditions and to give you eyes to see how he is at work. Thank him for his mercy when you are weak.

STUDY 3

FAITH OVER FEAR

Barak had every reason to fear Jabin's army. According to Judges 4:3, the Canaanite forces included nine hundred iron chariots. In the ancient world, chariots served as mobile firing platforms for archers. They were an advanced form of technology in ancient warfare that allowed the archers to rush in, spray the enemy with arrows, and quickly dart out of harm's way.[14] Sisera, the Canaanite general, also had the better position on the plain. His chariots could freely assault Barak's troops as they came down from the mountain. So it took great faith for Barak to charge Sisera.

Barak is not the only servant of God who felt afraid. Many years later, we read that David was afraid when his enemies harassed him. He wrote, "Fear and trembling grip me" (Psalm 55:5). Esther, a young Jewish woman who was married to the Persian king during the time of the exile, "was overcome with fear" when she learned about the edict to kill her people (Esther 4:4). Paul, the apostle who was so bold in sharing the message of the gospel, confided to the Corinthians, "I came to you in weakness, in fear, and in much trembling" (1 Corinthians 2:3).

Yet all these people overcame their weakness and fear with faith. How? They depended not on themselves but on the power of God. Paul said, "My goal is to know him and the power of his resurrection and the fellowship of his sufferings" (Philippians 3:10). When we are weak, fearful, or suffering in any other way, it's an opportunity for us to come to the end of ourselves and rest in the power of God—which brings us peace.

Fear in and of itself is not sin. We all feel afraid sometimes, and that's okay. It's what we do when fear assails us that determines whether we will live in chaos or walk in God's peace. So, when you are afraid, get still before God. Humble yourself in his presence. Remember that familiar passage: "Don't worry about anything, but in everything, through prayer and petition with thanksgiving, present your requests to God. And the peace of God, which surpasses all understanding, will guard your hearts and minds in Christ Jesus" (Philippians 4:6-7).

Fear doesn't have to be an obstacle to peace. Instead, it can be an opportunity for faith.

READ | Psalm 56:1-13; 1 Thessalonians 5:16-18; Philippians 3:3-11; Philippians 4:6-7

REFLECT

1. Survey time! Which of the following issues are causing fear or anxiety in your life right now? Mark any that are affecting you. In the space that follows, write down how you would like God to move in that situation to provide you with his peace.

☐ an uncertain relationship   ☐ decision you are pressured to make
☐ your job or career status   ☐ a situation in your family
☐ a health crisis or need   ☐ a certain financial challenge

You may be wondering if there is any hope at all for us to deal with our insecurities in a healthy way. There is, and you may be surprised to hear what it is. It's to pursue power. The kind of power that has been made available to us through Jesus—not the kind we attempt to gain for ourselves.[15]

2. Scholars believe that David wrote the words of Psalm 56 when he was on the run from King Saul and hiding out in the Philistine city of Gath. In this situation, David chose not to pursue his own power but God's power. What problems were causing David to fear? What did he resolve to do in spite of all those fears (see verses 1–4, 10–11)?

3. David not only asserted his faith in God when confronted with fear but also determined to worship the Lord and offer his thanksgiving (see verses 12–13). What does the apostle Paul say about the need for expressing gratitude to God in 1 Thessalonians 5:16–18?

Suffering, frailty, weakness, insecurity, instability, feeling overwhelmed, coming to the very end of ourselves—these all, through the lens of Christ, are not to be despised but cherished. They are the very things that connect us to him and to the power we are desperate for. When this connection takes place, we experience peace.[16]

4. In Philippians 3:3–11, Paul made it clear that losing our own power is the pathway to gaining Christ's power. How could coming to the end of yourself give you faith over fear?

5. Paul wrote, "Everything that was a gain to me, I have considered to be a loss because of Christ" (verse 7). Paul was completely focused on Jesus and the mission that he had been given of spreading the gospel. How did this focus help him to face his fear? What was Paul willing to do for the sake of obediently following after Christ?

PRAY | End your time in prayer. Ask God to let your fear be an opportunity for faith. Thank him today for his peace that passes understanding.

CONNECT & DISCUSS

Take today to connect with a group member and talk about some of the insights from this session. Use any of the prompts below to help guide your discussion.

What is one thing you learned this week about how humility can combat fear?

Which passage of Scripture you studied most applied to a situation you are facing?

What did you learn about yourself and how you tend to handle fear?

How does this week's study make you rethink your prayer life?

What will change in your life as a result of this study on not letting fear lead you?

CATCH UP & READ AHEAD

Use this time to go back and complete any of the study and reflection questions from previous days that you weren't able to finish. Make a note below of any questions you've had and reflect on any growth or personal insights you've gained.

Read chapters 6–7 in *The Hidden Peace* before the next group session. Use the space below to make note of anything that stands out to you or encourages you.

WEEK 3

BEFORE GROUP MEETING	Read chapters 6–7 in *The Hidden Peace* Read the Welcome section (page 42)
GROUP MEETING	Discuss the Connect questions Watch the video teaching for session 3 Discuss the questions that follow as a group Do the closing exercise and pray (pages 42–46)
STUDY 1	Complete the personal study (pages 49–51)
STUDY 2	Complete the personal study (pages 52–54)
STUDY 3	Complete the personal study (pages 55–57)
CONNECT & DISCUSS	Connect with someone in your group (page 58)
CATCH UP & READ AHEAD (BEFORE WEEK 4 GROUP MEETING)	Read chapters 8–9 in *The Hidden Peace* Complete any unfinished personal studies (page 59)

MANAGING YOUR AMBITIONS

Gideon said to them, "I will not rule over you, and my son will not rule over you; the LORD will rule over you." Then he said to them, "Let me make a request of you: Everyone give me an earring from his plunder."

JUDGES 8:23-24

WELCOME | READ ON YOUR OWN

There are many hurdles to experiencing peace in our lives. Fear is one of them, as we explored in the previous session. Another difficulty, which we will discuss in this session, is ambition.

What is ambition? *Merriam-Webster's Dictionary* describes it as "an ardent desire for rank, fame, or power."[17] We might think we don't have a problem with ambition, but it can be hidden deep in our hearts where we don't recognize it. When selfish ambition goes unchecked in our lives, it creates a recipe for chaos and unrest.

Gideon had a problem with ambition. We don't usually notice that when we read his story. He started out as the weakest in his clan and trusted God to win a great battle over the Midianites. But just because someone *starts out* well doesn't mean that he will *finish* well. Gideon didn't deal with the ambition in his heart, and it caused Israel to fall back into idolatry.

Any of us can fall prey to self-focused plans that can end up hurting others. Of course, it is not wrong to have desires. Many of our goals are totally right and blessed by God. But it's good for us to be on the lookout for pride that leads to unrestrained ambition. If we cultivate the soil of humility in our hearts by watching for and pulling out weeds of self-focused desire, we will safeguard the peace of God in our lives and in the lives of those around us.

CONNECT | 15 MINUTES

Get things started by discussing one of the following questions:

- What is something that spoke to your heart in last week's personal study that you would like to share with the group?

    — or —

- How do you view ambition? Do you see it as a positive or negative trait? Explain your response.

WATCH | 20 MINUTES

Now watch the video for this session. Below is an outline of the key points covered during the teaching. Record any key concepts that stand out to you.

OUTLINE

I. It is disorienting when someone says one thing but does the exact opposite.
   A. Gideon, whose story is at the center of Judges, was used mightily by God.
   B. He started out well, yet toward the end of his life, we find a disconnect between what he said and what he did. It all centered around his ambitions.
   C. There are five key moments in Gideon's life that shaped who he was and add to the confusion of some of the questionable decisions he made later on.

II. The five holy moments of humility in Gideon's life:
   A. Moment #1: When the Lord called Gideon to deliver Israel from the cycle of sin, Gideon responded with humility (see Judges 6:15).
   B. Moment #2: Gideon obeyed God and tore down his father's altar to Baal. He moved past his initial fears into obedience (see verses 25–27).
   C. Moment #3: Gideon asked God for confirmation through a test (see verses 33–39). God chose to go through Gideon's test as a gift of assurance.
   D. Moment #4: Gideon willingly accepted God's command to reduce the Israelite army to just three hundred men (see 7:6–8).
   E. Moment #5: God allowed Gideon to hear that the Midianite soldiers were afraid of the Israelites. Gideon then bowed before the Lord in worship (see verse 15).

III. We must watch for prideful ambitions that spoil the soil of humility in our lives.
   A. Gideon, as a judge, secured peace and stability and restored the joy of God's people. He not only heard God's instructions but also obeyed them.
   B. Gideon told the people, "The LORD will rule over you" (8:23). But then he asked the people for the spoils of war and used them to create an ephod.
   C. Although Gideon denied the kingship, he basically set himself up as a king by asking for gold, keeping the symbols of royalty, and creating the ephod.

IV. God used Gideon to restore peace, but the cost of Gideon's pride was great.
   A. The Midianites were subdued, and Israel had peace for forty years. But the people started the cycle of sin again by worshiping Gideon's ephod.
   B. Many people start out with a compass of humility that guides them in life but fail to cultivate that practice. Many people start well but do not finish well.
   C. We watch out for unrestrained ambition by keeping our focus on God and giving him the glory. Humility is God's gift that leads us out of cycles of sin.

NOTES

DISCUSS | 35 MINUTES

Now discuss what you just watched by answering the following questions.

1. The first holy moment in Gideon's life occurred when the Lord called him to deliver his people from the Midianites. Gideon responded to God's call by saying, "Please, Lord, how can I deliver Israel? Look, my family is the weakest in Manasseh, and I am the youngest in my father's family" (Judges 6:15). How did this demonstrate Gideon's humility before the Lord?

2. Ask someone to read aloud Judges 7:2. Another key holy moment in Gideon's life occurred when he agreed to go into battle against the Midianites with only three hundred men. What reason did God provide for asking Gideon to reduce the number of his men? What was God already watching out for when it came to the hearts and minds of his people?

3. After all the good that Gideon had done for the Israelites, it is little wonder that they wanted to elevate him to the status of king. Gideon said all the right things—proclaiming that only God would rule over them—but then did something wrong. How did his choice to take the spoils of war cause the entire nation of Israel to fall back into the cycle of sin?

4. Consider this statement from the teaching: "Humility is something that needs to be cultivated." What are some things that you have done to cultivate humility in your life?

5. So many people start well but are unable to finish well. Why do you think Gideon ultimately succumbed to pride? Why do you think it is so hard for us to stay humble for the long haul?

RESPOND | 10 MINUTES

Most of us don't deliberately set out to chase selfish ambition. It just creeps into our hearts when we fail to continually cultivate the soil of humility. If we aren't careful, pride can soon take root to disturb our peace and the peace of those we love. However, as Paul wrote, when we put on traits such as "compassion, kindness, humility, gentleness, and patience, bearing with one another and forgiving one another" (Colossians 3:12–13), it takes the focus off ourselves, our needs, and our ambitions. Take a few minutes on your own to honestly examine your desires in light of this truth. Use the questions below to help guide you in this reflection.

What is one desire you have that you believe God has given to you?

How could pride take advantage of this desire and turn it into unrestrained ambition?

What are some practical things you can do to cultivate humility in this matter and maintain the peace in your life that God desires for you to have?

PRAY | 10 MINUTES

End your time by praying together as a group. As you pray, ask God to give you a humble heart and to help you cultivate practices of loving and serving others that will help you stay humble. Ask if anyone has prayer requests, and then write down those requests so that you and your fellow group members can continue to pray about them in the week ahead.

SESSION THREE

PERSONAL STUDY

As you learned from Gideon's story in this week's group time, even those who start out with the best intentions can be waylaid by hidden plans and ambitions that get out of control. This is why it is so important for us to tend to our hearts, watching out for any pride and self-absorption that can cause us to veer off track and lose our humility. This week, you will have the opportunity to further explore what the Bible says about pride, unrestrained ambition, and the humility that protects us from these problems. As you work through the exercises, be sure to write down your responses to the questions, as you will be given a few minutes to share your insights at the start of the next session if you are doing this study with others. If you are reading *The Hidden Peace* alongside this study, first review chapters 6–7 in the book.

STARTING WELL

It is important to start well. For instance, in the National Football League, statistics show that a team that starts 0–2 has only an 11.5 percent chance of making the playoffs. For teams that start 0–3, the odds drop down to 2.5 percent.[18] NFL players know it is important to get out of the gate strong.

Gideon started well. As you discussed this week, when the Israelites were being oppressed by the Midianites, the Lord appeared to Gideon and instructed him to "go in the strength you have and deliver Israel from the grasp of Midian" (Judges 6:14). Gideon responded in humility, stating that his family was the weakest in the land and that he was the youngest of his family. The Lord assured Gideon that he would be with him and give him the victory.

When the Lord told Gideon to tear down his father's altar to Baal, Gideon was afraid, but he did it. As Gideon built an army, he felt uncertain and asked God to make a fleece wet and leave the ground dry—and then do the opposite—and the Lord answered his prayer.

When Gideon gathered more than thirty-two thousand troops, the Lord said, "You have too many. . . Israel might elevate themselves over me and say, 'I saved myself'" (Judges 7:2). As God whittled his army down to ten thousand, then down all the way to just three hundred men, Gideon held steady and trusted the Lord. The Israelites then surrounded the Midianites, blew their trumpets, shattered jars, and held up torches, shouting, "For the LORD and for Gideon!" (verse 18). The enemy soldiers, in a panic, turned on each other and were defeated.

Has God called you to do a task for him? If so, it is important to lay a strong foundation. When you start well—bowing low before your heavenly Father in humility and courageously obeying him like Gideon did—you will live in the power and peace of God.

READ | Judges 6:1–32; Galatians 5:22–23; James 4:10

REFLECT

1. According to Judges 6:1–11, what was the situation for Israel like at the time the Lord appeared to Gideon? How does this further explain Gideon's fear?

2. After Gideon tore down his father's altar to Baal and the Asherah pole next to it, how did the men of his city respond (see verses 28–30)? How does this highlight just how far the nation of Israel had fallen from worship of the Lord?

> Humility is the soil we need for cultivating Christian virtues. The soil of humility in our lives is the perfect place for the fruit of the Spirit to grow, be nurtured, and mature (Galatians 5). Every good farmer pays close attention to the condition of his soil, checking to see if outside forces have somehow corrupted it, because corrupted soil bears spoiled fruit, or no fruit. When pride is planted in the good soil of humility, it can corrupt the soil and derail us as we grow in godliness.[19]

3. When the Lord first appeared to Gideon, he called him a "valiant warrior" (6:12). There was something about the way Gideon was living his life that brought him to God's attention. What does Paul say in Galatians 5:22–23 that we should seek to cultivate in our lives? How will this help us to start well and keep our focus on Christ?

4. When have you found yourself in a situation where you felt that what God was asking you to do would potentially go against the culture of your family or friends? How did you choose to act in that situation . . . and what was the outcome of your actions?

The power of humility is the clarity it brings us. It allows us to see ourselves and others the way we ought to. When we see ourselves the right way, we're more secure and confident. We feel more joy and satisfaction. When we see people the right way, we can treat them well and build healthier relationships.[20]

5. There is power in humility. What are followers of Jesus instructed to do in James 4:10? What will the Lord do if we obey the command that is given to us in this verse?

PRAY | End your time in prayer. Ask the Lord to help you lay a foundation of humility in your life that will hold fast through whatever he calls you to do.

WATCH YOUR HEART

Most people don't think of themselves as proud. But pride isn't always easy to spot. Sometimes people can come across as kind, good, and gentle but at the root still have a sickness. This was true of Gideon. He started out by humbly serving, but Gideon had a problem lurking beneath the surface. This only became visible when he was tempted to promote himself.

As you discussed in this week's group time, after Gideon defeated the Midianites, the Israelites came to him and said, "Rule over us" (Judges 8:22). Gideon responded with apparent humility: "I will not rule over you . . . the LORD will rule over you" (verse 23). But then he made a request: "Everyone give me an earring from his plunder" (verse 24). The people agreed, and so Gideon received their ornaments, pendants, purple garments—the stuff of royalty. It was as if he had made himself king, but without the title.

The saddest part of the story is that Gideon took his gold and made an ephod—a vest-like garment worn by priests—and "all Israel prostituted themselves by worshiping it" (verse 27). Seriously? God had just delivered the people from years and years of oppression that had been caused by idol worship. Now they were immediately returning to the same sin! Gideon's hidden pride led to unrestrained ambition, which led to the people's idolatry.

Hidden pride operates in the heart behind closed doors. So we don't always know it is there until circumstances expose it. Given this, if we want to stay on the path of humility, we have to look honestly at our hearts and deal with any pride that we find there.

READ | Judges 8:22–27; Proverbs 16:18; Mark 7:21–23; Isaiah 2:17; Psalm 139:23–24

REFLECT

1. When have you found yourself tempted to move away from a good start because of a situation that exposed a hidden ambition? How did you respond in that situation?

One reason pride is so dangerous is that it has the ability to twist godly virtues into deadly, self-serving vices. On the outside it may look like we are living out the fruit of the Spirit, but on the inside, we are leveraging it to meet our own selfish ambition and vain conceit. *Love, joy, peace, patience, kindness, goodness, faithfulness, gentleness, and self-control are all great, as long as they serve a greater purpose—my self-exaltation.*[21]

2. Pride twisted Gideon's godly virtues into self-serving vices—and his family and the people of Israel paid the price. How did Gideon's decision to craft the ephod impact his household (see Judges 8:27)? How would it have marred the legacy he passed on to his children?

3. Look up the following passages that talk about pride. Next to each, write down what it says to you about the dangers of not walking in humility.

Proverbs 16:18	
Mark 7:21–23	
Isaiah 2:17	

4. The psalmist wrote, "The LORD is good and upright.... He leads the humble in what is right and teaches them his way" (Psalm 25:8–9). When we cultivate humility in our hearts, God leads us along the right paths. How could this have helped Gideon when he was presented with temptation? How could this help you when you face similar challenges?

> While we're not dealing with actual idols on pedestals today, many of us are dealing with self-absorption. In our hearts we are "lifting up ourselves," making ourselves the focal point, the authority, and the ultimate source for meeting our own needs.[22]

5. According to Psalm 139:23–24, what is the best way for you to find out if there is any hidden pride or "self-absorption" in your heart? How would it help you to avoid unrestrained ambition if you stayed on the "everlasting way"?

PRAY | End your time in prayer. Invite God to search your heart to reveal anything there that does not come from him. Then thank him for his willingness to do so.

FINISHING WELL

As a child, you might have heard the fable of "The Tortoise and the Hare." As the story goes, a tortoise and hare one day have a race. The hare sprints out of the gate and gets so far ahead of the tortoise that he decides to take a nap midway through the run. When he awakes, he finds that the tortoise—crawling slowly but steadily—has arrived at the finish line before him.

So many people are like the hare. They start well, but then—because of pride—they get distracted from their mission and stray off course. We've already seen that Gideon started well but ended badly. While God, in his mercy, gave Israel peace for forty years, Gideon's unrestrained ambition led to the people falling right back into the cycle of sin and idolatry.

The ultimate example of pride found in the Bible is that of Satan. Isaiah wrote of him, "You said to yourself, 'I will ascend to the heavens; I will set up my throne above the stars of God.' . . . But you will be brought down to Sheol into the deepest regions of the Pit" (Isaiah 14:13, 15). When God created the world, he set boundaries that people were not to cross. But Satan rebelled against God's plan, and in an effort to destroy God's creation and rule it himself, he deceived Adam and Eve into crossing those boundaries. He tempted them to do what he himself was doing: defy God and please self. What terrible destruction it caused.

The opposite of pride is humility. As Jonathan Edwards wrote, "Humility tends to prevent an aspiring and ambitious behavior amongst men."[23] The best example of humility is Jesus, who "humbled himself by becoming obedient to the point of death—even to death on a cross" (Philippians 2:8). Jesus died to redeem us from the awful damage caused by pride.

If you want to finish well, choose the path of humility. The way of pride ends only in destruction. But the way of humility leads to honor, life, and peace.

READ | Ezekiel 28:11–19; Philippians 2:3–8; Matthew 23:11–12; Philippians 2:9–11

REFLECT

1. Who do you know who finished a task well or finished their life well? What are some distinctive characteristics from that person's life that you would like to see in your own?

> Satan's splendor and beauty caused him to think of himself *a lot*—like, obsessively. Pride creates an over-elevated view of ourselves. It robs us of our self-awareness and tempts us to magnify ourselves and minimize everyone else. . . . Pride distorts our vision and corrupts the good soil of humility. This is exactly what happened to Satan.[24]

2. In Ezekiel 28:11–19, we read another passage about the fall of Satan. In Philippians 2:3–8, we read about the attitude that Jesus possessed. In the boxes below, list some of the qualities of pride and of humility that you find in each of these two passages.

Qualities of Pride (Ezekiel 28:15–19)	Qualities of Humility (Philippians 2:3–8)

3. When *pride*—the enemy of humility—invades the human heart, there is always some sort of cost. In Gideon's case, the cost was to his household and the Israelite people. How have you seen this play out in your life or in the life of someone you know?

4. According to Matthew 23:11–12, what will happen to those who exalt themselves? What will happen to those who humble themselves?

The beauty of humility is that it is where God breathes life into us. When we are in this posture, he swoops down from the heights of heaven to pick us up and elevate us with him as children of the King, placing us where we can experience true peace.[25]

5. According to Philippians 2:9–11, what was the end result of Jesus finishing well? How does this encourage you to want to be like him?

PRAY | End your time in prayer. Ask God to give you the same attitude as Jesus Christ and to help you not only start well but also finish well.

CONNECT & DISCUSS

Take today to connect with a group member and talk about some of the insights from this session. Use any of the prompts below to help guide your discussion.

What is one new thing you learned this week about pride or ambition?

What area of your life did this week's study challenge you to grow in?

How will the challenge to combat pride and cultivate greater humility affect your prayer life?

What about Jesus' example of humility most ministers to you?

What verse or passage of Scripture from this week's personal studies will you memorize to help you not just *start* well but also *finish* well?

CATCH UP & READ AHEAD

Use this time to go back and complete any of the study and reflection questions from previous days that you weren't able to finish. Make a note below of any questions you've had and reflect on any growth or personal insights you've gained.

Read chapters 8–9 in *The Hidden Peace* before the next group session. Use the space below to make note of anything that stands out to you or encourages you.

WEEK 4

BEFORE GROUP MEETING	Read chapters 8-9 in *The Hidden Peace* Read the Welcome section (page 62)
GROUP MEETING	Discuss the Connect questions Watch the video teaching for session 4 Discuss the questions that follow as a group Do the closing exercise and pray (pages 62-66)
STUDY 1	Complete the personal study (pages 69-71)
STUDY 2	Complete the personal study (pages 72-74)
STUDY 3	Complete the personal study (pages 75-77)
CONNECT & DISCUSS	Connect with someone in your group (page 78)
CATCH UP & READ AHEAD (BEFORE WEEK 5 GROUP MEETING)	Read chapters 10-12 in *The Hidden Peace* Complete any unfinished personal studies (page 79)

SESSION FOUR

UNTANGLING YOUR PAIN

Jephthah the Gileadite was a valiant warrior, but he was the son of a prostitute, and Gilead was his father.

JUDGES 11:1

61

WELCOME | READ ON YOUR OWN

Pain is an unwelcome companion. It comes in many shapes and sizes and at different times in our lives, but it always leaves behind unanswered questions and heartbreaking challenges. Pain, like fear and ambition, can get in the way of the humility that brings us peace.

In the previous session, we saw how the Israelites fell back into a cycle of sin during the time of Gideon. The judges Tola and Jair followed. The Israelites then came under attack by a group known as the Ammonites. This time, they didn't cry out to the Lord. They went straight to a man named Jephthah and asked him to lead them in fighting the enemy.

Jephthah had endured a painful upbringing. He was the son of a prostitute and had been driven out of his family by his brothers, who didn't want him to share in the family inheritance. Jephthah fled to the land of Tob, where he led a band of renegades. Now the people wanted Jephthah back, for he was a trained, seasoned, and mighty warrior.

Perhaps you resonate with Jephthah's story. Maybe you are also suffering from the loneliness of rejection or isolation. You feel as if you have been exiled. But know that God can use your pain to bring about peace—even for those who have hurt you. Humility might not seem like an obvious path to healing and peace, but it is the gateway to having a heart that can listen, reflect, and be restored. God redeemed Jephthah's pain, and he can redeem yours.

CONNECT | 15 MINUTES

Get things started by discussing one of the following questions:

- What is something that spoke to your heart in last week's personal study that you would like to share with the group?

  — or —

- What is an early memory you have of feeling hurt by someone?

WATCH | 20 MINUTES

Now watch the video for this session. Below is an outline of the key points covered during the teaching. Record any key concepts that stand out to you.

OUTLINE

I. We all have a bit of "it's complicated" in our pasts that can derail our peace.
   A. Jephthah had a complicated past. He is introduced as a warrior trained in upper-class combat (Hebrew *gibbor chayil*). But he was also the son of a prostitute.
   B. The author of Judges states, "Gilead was his father" (Judges 11:1). His father is personified as the land of Gilead. His connection was to land and not his father.
   C. Jephthah's brothers kicked him out, and he was exiled to the land of Tob. In Hebrew, the name means "good," but there was *nothing* good about that land.

II. God intervened into Jephthah's story and redeemed his broken and painful past.
   A. We may find our stories reflected in Jephthah's past—isolation, rejection, separation from loved ones. There is nothing good about what we're experiencing.
   B. Yet we find God was redeeming Jephthah's story. It began when the Israelites—many of whom had exiled him—begged Jephthah to be their rescuer.
   C. Jephthah told them that if God gave him the victory over the Ammonites, he would be their leader. His humility in this moment would lead to Israel's peace.
   D. Jephthah repeated his terms in the presence of the Lord. Humility is found in God's presence.

III. Sadly, the complication in Jephthah's story is not limited to his early years.
   A. In Jephthah's dialogue with the king of Ammon, he recounts that God had given Israel victory at every turn. But he mixes pagan ideas with his views on God.
   B. Jephthah had general knowledge about God, but he did not have an intimate understanding of the Lord. He mixed cult religions with his faith in Yahweh.
   C. We can also be tempted to mix culture into our faith. We make compromises, mixing what we know to be true about God with what the world says is true.

IV. Our posture of humility influences our thoughts, words, and eventual outcomes.
   A. Jephthah ended up compromising his humble faith in the God of Israel for an openness to pagan religion—which led to great personal disaster.
   B. Humility isn't something we start with and then move on from. Humility is the soil of the Christian life, and all other fruits of the Spirit flow from it.
   C. We must cultivate the soil of humility, pulling out the competing stories from our pasts and the values from our culture that can lead us into pride.

NOTES

DISCUSS | 35 MINUTES

Now discuss what you just watched by answering the following questions.

1. Jephthah endured a painful upbringing. He was the son of a prostitute who was hated and exiled by his brothers. Jephthah fled to the land of Tob, which in Hebrew means "pleasing, good, or pleasant."[26] But nothing good happened to Jephthah in the land of Tob. When have you thought that a change in your life would bring about good—but it did not?

2. When the Ammonites invaded Israel, the same community who had exiled Jephthah came to him and asked him to be their commander. How would you feel if the people who once rejected you now wanted you to come and help them? How would you respond?

3. Jephthah based the conditions of his leadership of the Israelite people on his awareness of God and his understanding that victory would only come through the presence, power, and authority of the Lord. How does this demonstrate Jephthah's humility? What is the significance of him repeating these terms in the presence of the Lord at Mizpah?

4. Jephthah had general knowledge about God, but his dialogue with the king of the Ammonites reveals that his understanding of Yahweh and his people was incomplete. How was he influenced by the culture? Why is it so dangerous to mix what the world tells us is true with what the Word of God says is true?

5. Humility is like good soil for the Christian soul. It is the foundation from which fruit of the Spirit like peace, kindness, goodness, and gentleness take root and grow. What are you doing to cultivate this soil? What are some of the "weeds," or faulty teachings of the world, that you need to remove from the soil of your heart?

RESPOND | 10 MINUTES

It's not easy to respond well to pain. When someone hurts us, our natural tendency is to lash out, run away, or fall into grief and bitterness. But when we humble ourselves before the Lord and quiet ourselves before him, we can begin to hear the healing and redeeming words that he has to say. Take a few minutes on your own to consider how you typically respond when someone causes you pain. Use the questions below to help guide you in this reflection.

What is something painful from your past that has been hard to move past?

What are some wrong ways and right ways that you have responded to this pain?

What are some practical things you can do to come humbly before God and honestly ask about your hurt so that you can move toward healing and peace?

PRAY | 10 MINUTES

End your time by praying together as a group. As you pray, ask God to help you be honest with him about your pain and to believe that he truly wants to redeem whatever hurtful thing you have experienced. Ask if anyone has prayer requests, and then write down those requests so that you and your fellow group members can continue to pray about them in the week ahead.

PERSONAL STUDY

In this week's group time, you saw how Jephthah endured great personal pain in his childhood and early years. However, God was able to redeem his past, and through Jephthah the Lord freed the Israelites from the Ammonites and brought about peace in the land. Unfortunately, Jephthah's upbringing in Tob had led to him being influenced by pagan culture, and this in turn led to him making decisions that proved disastrous for his family. This week, you will have the opportunity to look at a few verses to see what the Bible says about our pain and how humility can bring about healing and peace. As you work through the exercises, be sure to write down your responses to the questions, as you will be given a few minutes to share your insights at the start of the next session if you are doing this study with others. If you are reading *The Hidden Peace* alongside this study, first review chapters 8–9 in the book.

HUMILITY BRINGS HEALING

When you have been hurt, where do you turn for comfort? Some of us talk to a friend. Others escape into a movie or book. Some of us drown our sorrows in other self-medicating avenues. It is doubtful that many of us would say, "I find comfort in humility." Perhaps this is because the world views humility as a weakness. Humility is equated with a low sense of self-esteem or a lack of confidence. But the truth is that humility is the path to strength and courage.

Jephthah, the son of a prostitute, had been spurned and cast out of his family. When the elders from Gilead, his homeland, later came to him and asked him to be their commander, he did not avoid the pain he had felt in the past. "Didn't you hate me and drive me out of my father's family?" he asked. "Why then have you come to me now when you're in trouble?" (Judges 11:7). Humility faces facts honestly and sees things as they are.

Jephthah could have then continued, "I won't have anything to do with you," or, "You owe me an apology." But instead, he saw his people's plight and responded in humility. "If you are bringing me back to fight the Ammonites and the LORD gives them to me, I will be your leader" (verse 9). Jephthah allowed God to be his vindicator and his healer.

When Jephthah returned to Gilead, he repeated his terms in the presence of the Lord. As we noted in this week's teaching, it is in the presence of God that we know who we truly are. Jephthah saw God and, in return, God saw Jephthah and exalted him to a place of leadership.

God can use our pain to grow and strengthen us. When we humbly turn to the Lord for comfort, he will order our circumstances and exalt us for his own glory.

READ | Judges 11:1–11; Proverbs 22:4; Luke 18:9–14

REFLECT

1. What elements of Jephthah's painful past resonates with your own story? Why those particular elements?

> Instead of leaving us unstable and weak, humility makes us steadier and stronger. Instead of squashing down our strengths and potential, it helps the best of who we are flourish. It helps us have healthy, fulfilling relationships. And it gives us confidence to face our fears and courage to walk through our hurts.[27]

2. The world tends to define humility as weakness, but in Proverbs 22:4 we are told that humility results in wealth, honor, and life. When you think of the word *humility*, do your thoughts align more with the world's way of defining it or God's way? Why?

3. In Judges 11:7, we see that Jephthah was honest about his pain in his response to the Gilead elders. How does it help you to know that humility doesn't mean covering up your pain but instead honestly facing what happened? (Note: this doesn't make room for attacking those who hurt you but rather for being truthful about the pain they caused you.)

> [Humility] is the turning point of managing fear differently in our hearts. It is what flows out of humanity when we (1) see God as he truly is, (2) see ourselves in light of who God is, and (3) see others as God does. Cultivating humility also helps us see every situation and circumstance as something God rules over and can bring good out of.[28]

4. An attitude of humility opens our hearts and allows God to bring healing and understanding to our past hurts. How would humility help you see more accurately in each of these areas?

See that God knows your situation	
See that God cares about your pain	
See that God will bring good from it	

5. In the parable that Jesus told in Luke 18:9–14, how does Jesus make it clear that humility is not weakness but, in reality, a gateway to strength and blessing?

PRAY | End your time in prayer. Bring any current hurts that you are feeling before God. Ask him to help you find comfort in his presence and bring his healing and restoration in your life.

BEWARE THE MIXTURE

Jephthah's story is complicated. On the one hand, he was a valiant warrior who took up God's assignment to deliver the Israelites from oppression. His speech to the Ammonite king, in which he refuted his opponent's claims that the Israelites had seized their land when they came out of Egypt, revealed that he had an understanding of the Israelites' history and how God had intervened. But as noted in this week's teaching, some of the events that Jephthah related appear to be out of order. There are also others that appear to be wrong. For instance, there is no other mention in Scripture of the Israelites sending messengers to Moab (see Judges 11:17).

This could very well be a clue that Jephthah had incomplete knowledge about God and his people. Biblical scholars have also noted that Jephthah seemed to identify faith in Yahweh with the practices of the gods of the surrounding nations. This becomes evident when, in an attempt to ensure God will give him the victory, he makes a rash vow that if he is triumphant over the Ammonites, he will offer the first person who comes out of his house as a sacrifice to the Lord (see verses 30–31). Jephthah evidently didn't realize that God had made it clear that Israel was to reject pagan practices such as human sacrifice (see Deuteronomy 18:9–13).

Jephthah's faith in God had evidently been mixed with erroneous ideas that he had picked up while living in the land of Tob. As one scholar notes, "The notion of human sacrifice was all but universal among ancient nations, and it was especially prevalent among the Syrians, among whom Jephthah had lived for so many years."[29] Jephthah's faith in God was real. But even those who love God can make grievous mistakes if they allow their culture to infiltrate their faith. In Jephthah's case, as we will see, the result of this "mixing" was tragic.

Jesus told his followers that while they were in the world, they were not of the world (see John 17:16). This is true of us today. When we mix God's truth with the world's sense of truth, we end up with an incomplete and erroneous view of the Lord.

READ | Judges 11:12–28; Romans 12:2–3; 2 Corinthians 6:14–18

REFLECT

1. Time for another quick survey. Which of the following things in our culture today, if you were to give them free rein and access to your life, would negatively influence your faith? Number them in the order in which you think they tempt you the most.

____ social media	____ food
____ entertainment	____ politics
____ buying things	____ debating others
____ hobbies	____ work
____ sports	____ travel

2. What is your overall impression of Jephthah and his understanding of his people's history in Judges 11:12–28? What aspects about God's nature does he absolutely get right?

> Humility is fundamentally an intimate awareness of the magnitude of our sin and the magnificence of God's grace. If we are not first captivated by an awareness of who God truly is and who we are in light of him, the humble life is impossible.[30]

3. Humility compels us to focus our attention on God and learn about his truths in his Word. Seen in this light, how does humility protect you from buying into the lies and half-truths of this world? What are the benefits of staying focused on God through humility?

4. What did Paul advise us to do in Romans 12:2–3? What connection do you see
 between godly humility and avoiding the mindset of the world?

Awareness is a beautiful thing because it brings about proper orientation.
We stand in wonder at the infinite and great God who, in a breath, brought
about all creation. The kindness of a God who chose to breathe life into hu-
mans. The never-ending love of a God who sent his own Son to pay a price
we owed, dying a death we deserved, all so we could receive his righteous-
ness and join his family.[31]

5. Awareness of God's truths, and acting on those truths, keeps us from the con-
 sequences of buying into the deceptions of the world. According to 2 Corinthians 6:14–18, what promise do we have from God if we choose to come out from
 the world and be separate?

PRAY | End your time in prayer. Ask God to help you cultivate humility in your life
so you can know his truths, apply them to your life, and be separate from the world.

STUDY 3

CULTIVATE THE SOIL

Even when we are doing our best to please God, we often mess up. Why is that? A thought from South African pastor Andrew Murray sheds some light: "Humility is the only soil in which virtue takes root; a lack of humility is the explanation of every defect and failure."[32]

Tending to the soil of humility in our lives should be front and center. The minute we lose our humility, things such as fear, pride, ambition, and pain take hold. This is what happened to Jephthah. He handled his past with humility and humbly embraced the role that God assigned to him. But then he allowed uncertainty to displace humility and tried to bargain with God to secure victory. The end result of that decision would be disastrous.

Jesus once told his followers a parable about a farmer who sowed some seed. Some of the seed fell on the path and was gobbled up by birds. Some fell on rocky ground and didn't take root. Some fell among thorns and got choked out. But some fell on good soil and produced fruit: "Some a hundred, some sixty, and some thirty times what was sown" (Matthew 13:8).

Jesus explained that the seed in his story represented knowledge of the kingdom of God. Some hear the word but don't try to understand it, which allows the enemy to come and steal away the seed. Others hear the word but don't cultivate it in their hearts, which leads to the quick death of the seed. Others hear the word but allow the world to choke out its truths. But some hear the word and cultivate it, and their lives produce an abundant harvest for God.

If Jephthah had cultivated humility and sought a better understanding of God, he would have been able to recognize areas in his life that were going to cause chaos and needed to be rooted out. Humility must be tended. What chaos-causing habits, attitudes, or relationships are crowding the soil of humility in your life? Pull them out, and experience God's lasting peace.

READ | Matthew 11:28–30; Luke 1:26–38; Luke 1:46–55; John 13:12–15

REFLECT

1. How are you doing at cultivating humility in your life? What is one thing you still need to pull from your life to help you stay humble before God?

2. Jesus' words in Matthew 11:28–30 are filled with rich promises for anyone seeking to nurture humility. Read the passage and then answer the following questions. Circle the phrases that speak to you the most in your current situation.

What is Jesus' first command?	
How does he describe those who need peace?	
What will he do for us?	
What is Jesus' second command?	
What is his third command?	
How did Jesus describe himself?	
What did he say we will find?	
How does he describe his yoke and his burden?	

3. In Luke 1:26–38, the angel Gabriel visited Mary and told her that she would give birth to the Messiah. How did Mary respond? How does her response reveal a cultivated humility?

> Mary's song was informed by the humility she'd cultivated in her life. . . . It seems almost impossible to rejoice in God, glorify him for his greatness, anticipate his continued goodness, and exalt him for his faithfulness without a deep-rooted humility. . . . In Mary's case the song of praise was a response. I have a suspicion that Mary reflected on that song as the years went on.[33]

4. How did Mary describe herself in her song of praise to God (see verse 48)? Based on Mary's song, how does God respond to those who walk in humility?

> Humility truly is a fundamental aspect of life with Jesus. As we're united with him, it's the oxygen we breathe. It's the clothing we're always wearing. It's the soil we're rooted in. We become a humble person, just like he was. This also means that humility should be the fragrance that marks every Christian virtue.[34]

5. In John 13:12–15, Jesus modeled humility for his disciples by washing their feet. What was Jesus teaching them in this moment about cultivating the soil of humility in their hearts?

PRAY | End your time in prayer. Ask God to help you stay focused on him so you can maintain a spirit of humility that will produce good fruit for God's kingdom.

CONNECT & DISCUSS

Take today to connect with a group member and talk about some of the insights from this session. Use any of the prompts below to help guide your discussion.

What is one new thing you learned this week about how God can heal your pain?

What did you like most about Jephthah's story? What did you like the least?

What did you learn from Jephthah's story about the healing God brings when you exercise humility and forgive those who have caused you pain?

What is one way that you will be careful not to let false ideas from the culture around you infiltrate your faith?

What is one practical thing that you can do to cultivate humility in your life on a daily basis?

CATCH UP & READ AHEAD

Use this time to go back and complete any of the study and reflection questions from previous days that you weren't able to finish. Make a note below of any questions you've had and reflect on any growth or personal insights you've gained.

Read chapters 10–12 in *The Hidden Peace* before the next group session. Use the space below to make note of anything that stands out to you or encourages you.

WEEK 5

BEFORE GROUP MEETING	Read chapters 10–12 in *The Hidden Peace* Read the Welcome section (page 82)
GROUP MEETING	Discuss the Connect questions Watch the video teaching for session 5 Discuss the questions that follow as a group Do the closing exercise and pray (pages 82–86)
STUDY 1	Complete the personal study (pages 89–91)
STUDY 2	Complete the personal study (pages 92–94)
STUDY 3	Complete the personal study (pages 95–97)
CONNECT & DISCUSS	Connect with someone in your group (page 98)
CATCH UP & READ AHEAD (BEFORE WEEK 6 GROUP MEETING)	Read chapters 13–15 in *The Hidden Peace* Complete any unfinished personal studies (page 99)

GOD ALWAYS SEES YOU

*God has chosen what is foolish in the world
to shame the wise, and God has chosen what
is weak in the world to shame the strong.*

1 CORINTHIANS 1:27

WELCOME | READ ON YOUR OWN

Sometimes we find ourselves in a humble position not as a result of our own actions but because of the actions of others. Maybe we are picked on by a bully, or our ideas are shot down, or someone we thought was a friend turns on us. This is when we really have to decide whether we will embrace the humility of heart that will strengthen us to rise above our feelings of insignificance and be used by God for his glorious purposes.

In the ancient world, women typically had few to no rights and often found themselves in humble positions. Yet throughout the book of Judges, we find God placing women in important roles and using them in his plans for Israel. In a world dominated by men, God was revealing that he values those who are overlooked, unwanted, and oppressed.

In fact, God is drawn to weakness. He loves widows and orphans. He cares about lonely people. He is concerned about the poor and the sick and those who have no one else to help them. We see this again and again in both the Old and the New Testaments.

Our weaknesses don't disqualify us from being used by God. Yes, it is painful when someone overlooks us or overrules us. But God sees us. If we keep our hearts humble and respond to him in obedience instead of allowing others to hold us back, he will use us in amazing ways, fill us with his sense of worth, and use us to bless the people around us.

CONNECT | 15 MINUTES

Get things started by discussing one of the following questions:

- What is something that spoke to your heart in last week's personal study that you would like to share with the group?

  — or —

- When have you seen someone being overlooked or rejected by other people in society?

WATCH | 20 MINUTES

Now watch the video for this session. Below is an outline of the key points covered during the teaching. Record any key concepts that stand out to you.

OUTLINE

I. An overlooked aspect of Judges is the presence of women in important positions.

   A. The ancient world was dominated by men, yet God chose in this book (and throughout Scripture) to make visible the innate dignity and worth of women.

   B. This forced the nations around Israel to consider this God who used unlikely people in unexpected ways to accomplish his incredibly grand purposes.

   C. The women in Judges were not just aware of God's purposes but also obedient to doing what God called them to do. Hiding in plain sight is humility.

II. Four women stand out as examples of humility, courage, and obedience.

   A. Deborah was a prophetess (mouthpiece) of God and accompanied Barak into battle. Neither of these were typical roles for women in that day.

   B. Jael killed Sisera, the general of Canaan, by luring him into her tent. As Deborah had prophesied, she was credited with killing this enemy of God's people.

   C. Jephthah's daughter accepted the outcome of her father's mistake.

      1. Jephthah vowed to sacrifice whoever came out of his house when he returned. His only daughter came out of the home to greet him.

      2. She refused to take her father's blame for the mistake that he had made.

      3. She demonstrated strength, courage, and humility in this tragic story.

   D. An angel told Samson's mother that she would give birth to a son.

      1. It is significant that the angel shows up to her instead of Samson's father.

      2. Her husband, Manoah, then prays for the angel to return to *both* of them.

      3. But the angel again shows up to her . . . a humorous moment in Scripture.

      4. God chose to first reveal the miracle of Samson's birth to his mother.

III. These women—in their selflessness, courage, and faith—brought about peace.

   A. Paul states that God chooses "what is foolish in the world to shame the wise, and . . . what is weak in the world to shame the strong" (1 Corinthians 1:27).

   B. The stories of these four women in Judges serve as a reminder that God always sees us and cares about us. They are just the tip of the iceberg of the humble women God has used throughout human history.

   C. God sent Jesus in an act of humility to take on the sin of the world. When we humbly receive God's gift, we will sleep in peace and live in safety.

NOTES

DISCUSS | 35 MINUTES

Now discuss what you just watched by answering the following questions.

1. What are several of the important responsibilities the Lord gave to Deborah? How does this encourage you to know that God can use anyone for his purposes?

2. The women of Judges demonstrated humility by not only being *aware* of God's purposes but also by *acting* on what God had called them to do. How do we see this in the story of Deborah? How did Jael exhibit humility and courage when she killed Sisera?

3. Jephthah believed in Yahweh but was open to the possibility of other gods. The foolish vow he made to sacrifice "whoever comes out the doors of my house to greet me when I return safely" (Judges 11:31) shows that his heart was compromised. How did his daughter demonstrate strength, humility, and courage in her response to her father's foolish vow?

4. The mother of Samson is introduced in the Bible as a woman who "was unable to conceive and had no children" (Judges 13:2). She would have endured great social shame, for often a woman's barrenness was attributed to some hidden wrong, sin, or flaw.[35] How did the Lord reveal that he saw this woman's plight and cared enough to do something about it?

5. Deborah, Jael, Jephthah's daughter, and Samson's mother were in humble positions in society but also had humble hearts before God. How would you describe the difference between being involuntarily placed in a humble position and having a humble heart?

RESPOND | 10 MINUTES

Every person has experienced the feeling of helplessness that comes from being marginalized, rejected, or ostracized. But the stories of the women in Judges reveals that other people's attitudes toward us don't have to define us. God sees us and wants to empower us and use us for his glory. Take a few minutes on your own to consider your feelings about times you have been marginalized or overlooked. Use the questions below to help guide you in this reflection.

How do you feel when someone dismisses or belittles you? How do you respond?

How can knowing that God sees you and understands your situation help you to respond in humility when you feel slighted or overlooked?

How could your situation become a pathway to helping and encouraging others?

PRAY | 10 MINUTES

End your time by praying together as a group. As you pray, ask God to help you realize that he does see you and wants to give you the humility, strength, and peace you need to fulfill his purposes for your life. Ask if anyone has prayer requests, and then write them down so that you and your fellow group members can continue to pray about them in the week ahead.

SESSION FIVE

PERSONAL STUDY

The stories of the women in Judges reveal that God uses the unlikely, overlooked, and marginalized to fulfill his purposes. Deborah was a prophet and judge. Jael took out an enemy commander. Jephthah's daughter provided a model for humility. Samson's mother heard the voice of God, believed, and obeyed his commands. This week, you will have the opportunity to look at a few other verses in Scripture to see how God views those who are lonely, forgotten, neglected, and overlooked. As you work through these exercises, be sure to write down your responses to the questions, as you will be given a few minutes to share your insights at the start of the next session if you are doing this study with others. If you are reading *The Hidden Peace* alongside this study, first review chapters 10–12 in the book.

GOD CAN USE YOU

Israel at the time of the judges was a highly patriarchal society. The father (or oldest male) of a family made all the decisions that affected the entire household. A girl was raised to obey her father without question, and when she was old enough to marry, she was expected to obey her husband in the same way. If she were divorced (which only the husband could initiate) or widowed, she typically returned to her father's house to live. Women were expected to spend their days as housewives and mothers who supported their husbands in all matters.[36]

Deborah was an exception to this rule. She was not only a prophetess of God but also a judge who conducted legal proceedings in the land. As the Bible relates, "She would sit under the palm tree of Deborah between Ramah and Bethel in the hill country of Ephraim, and the Israelites went up to her to settle disputes" (Judges 4:5). While positions of leadership in that time were usually filled by men, especially in matters of war, Deborah had the authority to go to a warrior like Barak and say, "Go, deploy the troops on Mount Tabor" (verse 6).

When Barak asked Deborah to ride with him into battle, she would have been justified in responding, "It is not my role to go with you to war." In fact, accompanying Barak would have required her to sacrifice some of her everyday responsibilities in the civil life of Israel. But instead, Deborah courageously rose to the occasion and said, "I will gladly go with you" (verse 9). Her humility was revealed in her willingness to do whatever God asked of her.

God is looking for humble people whom he can use for his plans and purposes. He doesn't care who society has deemed "usable" or "unusable." Rather, he extends the invitation to *everyone* to follow him, serve him, and be used to do incredible things for him.

READ | Judges 4:6–10; Judges 5:24–27; Matthew 10:29–31

REFLECT

1. What is one thing that you sense God has been calling you to do? In what ways might a sense of feeling overlooked or rejected be keeping you from stepping out in obedience?

2. When Barak asked Deborah to go with him into battle, what was her attitude (see Judges 4:9)? How would it help you overcome feelings of insecurity or insignificance to have the same faith-filled response toward whatever God is asking you to do?

Paul wrote that we are to "adopt the same attitude as that of Jesus Christ" (Philippians 2:5). The word adopt is telling us to take purposeful action toward becoming something we currently are not. It also leaves us with a sense of responsibility. It's up to us to decide to join Jesus on the journey of humility.[37]

3. According to Judges 5:24–27, how did Jael take purposeful action when Sisera approached her tent? How is Jael described by Deborah in verse 24?

4. In moments when you feel overlooked or discouraged, how can the words of Matthew 10:29–31 give you peace and remind you that God sees you?

One of the most practical things you can do to foster a lifestyle of humility is invest in your emotional, physical, and spiritual health. Jesus repeatedly withdrew to lonely places, and a bunch of those times he walked up a hill (physical). Other times he rested (emotional). And other times he prayed (spiritual). . . . Today is a great day to build some time into your schedule to sneak away and begin to construct some routines of humility. For Jesus it was prayer, walks, solitude, and rest. The same could be true for us.[38]

5. How often do you get away to a lonely place to spend time with Jesus? How could doing this regularly help you foster a lifestyle of humility that will result in increased courage, faith, and obedience to God?

PRAY | End your time in prayer. Ask God to help you overcome any sense of insignificance placed on you by others and instead to go forward in his strength.

GOD KNOWS YOUR NAME

We can only imagine how Jephthah's daughter felt when she learned that her father had promised to sacrifice whoever first came out his door to greet him on his return from battle. It must have taken her breath away to realize in a moment that all her dreams—to marry, have children, keep a home of her own—were suddenly shattered. Amazingly, she responded with humility to the pain inflicted on her by someone who should have protected her.

Samson's mother, in a world in which a woman's sense of purpose and worth was tied to having children, had empty arms and a broken heart. We don't know how many years she had hoped for a child, but it was long enough for her to be labeled "barren." We can likewise only imagine how *she* felt when the angel of the Lord said, "Although you are unable to conceive and have no children, you will conceive and give birth to a son" (Judges 13:3). Afterward, she and her husband humbly offered a sacrifice to the Lord.

God notices those with a humble heart. Jesus once went to the temple in Jerusalem and watched as the rich people dropped their extravagant offerings into the treasury. But then he looked and saw a poor widow dropping in two tiny coins. "'Truly I tell you,' he said, 'this poor widow has put in more than all of them. For all these people have put in gifts out of their surplus, but she out of her poverty has put in all she had to live on'" (Luke 21:1–4).

We don't know the names of Jephthah's daughter, or Samson's mother, or the widow whose action impressed Jesus at the temple. But God does. He sees those who are alone, grieving, or outside society—and he invites them to cast their cares on him. People may not know what you are going through, but God knows exactly who you are. He will help you.

READ | Ephesians 1:3–6; Judges 11:34–40; Judges 13:2–24; 1 Peter 5:6–7

REFLECT

1. What does Paul say in Ephesians 1:3–6 that God chose to do on our behalf?

Throughout the Old Testament, the God-centered concept of humility is *positive*. This would have been shocking for the Greco-Roman world (New Testament time period)—just as it is for us now, in our culture. The running theme throughout the Old Testament is a gracious God lovingly choosing the lowly and weak, saving them, and lifting them up.[39]

2. Most people, when confronted with the horrible reality that Jephthah told his daughter, would have collapsed in anguish. How does the response of Jephthah's daughter in Judges 11:34–40 reveal a countercultural humility that could strengthen the faith of others?

When we see humility from a God-first perspective, it will place us in the safe, secure, and strong hands of the Creator of the universe. However, if we view humility through a human-first perspective, it will lead us to rely on our own feeble and fragile strength.[40]

3. According to Judges 13:19–23, how did the words of Samson's mother's contrast with the words of his father? In what ways did her words reflect a God-first perspective?

4. As best as you can tell from the stories of Jephthah's daughter and Samson's mother told in Scripture, how did they respond to the following emotions?

Emotion	Jephthah's daughter	Samson's mother
Shock		
Hurt from someone they loved		
Loss of a dream		
Loneliness		

5. Both Jephthah's daughter and Samson's mother lived out the commands of 1 Peter 5:6–7. How would applying these same verses in your life change your outlook and give you the courage to trust God for your own needs?

PRAY | End your time in prayer. Thank God that he sees you and knows your name. Ask him to help you cast your cares on him in faith when you feel alone.

STUDY 3

CONDUITS OF PEACE

When we experience "the peace of God, which surpasses all understanding" (Philippians 4:7), we become conduits of that peace to others. Just consider the Samaritan woman who met Jesus at a well. Jesus' acceptance of her, and his offer to give her living water, forever changed her life. She was filled with God's peace and became a conduit of that peace to others. She ran to her community, where she had previously been shamed due to her immoral lifestyle, and told the people about the Messiah. This led to many receiving the gospel of peace.

God isn't looking for rich, smart, educated, or well-connected people to touch others with his peace. He is looking for people with hearts like Deborah, Jael, Jephthah's daughter, and Samson's mother—the ones whom society tends to overlook. It's not that God doesn't use people who are rich, smart, educated, or well-connected, but those aren't the qualifications for serving the Lord. God uses humble people who have been so changed by him, and who love him so much in return, that their lives are a walking testimony to his grace and peace.

The apostle Paul wrote, "God has chosen what is foolish in the world to shame the wise, and God has chosen what is weak in the world to shame the strong. God has chosen what is insignificant and despised in the world—what is viewed as nothing—to bring to nothing what is viewed as something, so that no one may boast in his presence" (1 Corinthians 1:27–29). Have you ever felt foolish, weak, insignificant, or despised? If so, be comforted! God sees you.

Jesus said, "Each tree is known by its own fruit. Figs aren't gathered from thornbushes, or grapes picked from a bramble bush. A good person produces good out of the good stored up in his heart" (Luke 6:44–45). Turn your insecurities into humility and your humility into faith, and you will become a channel of God's peace that overflows to everyone around you.

READ | John 4:1-42; John 14:27; John 16:7

REFLECT

1. Why was the Samaritan woman surprised when Jesus talked with her (see John 4:6–9)? How did Jesus' compassion give her the courage to be a conduit of God's peace to a society that had shamed her for the immoral lifestyle she had lived (see verses 28–30, 39–42)?

> We can control where we find our security, the tools we bring into every situation, and the way we respond to hard moments. We can allow humility to protect our hearts in the midst of the inevitable humiliations of life. We can let God equip us to face them and get through them. And as we do, we'll become stronger and better for it.[41]

2. How do Jesus' words in John 14:27 assure you that you can overcome the fear of what others think of you and embrace the peace of God?

3. How has God touched you with his love and lifted you up after others have knocked you down? How could that experience help others who have also been knocked down?

> Whenever you're dealing with insecurity, instability, or just the unknown, know that there is a way forward. There's a way to face your fears, weakness, and pain and stay rooted in humility. Now, that way forward is not easy. In our moments of weakness, we need help—someone to meet us in our struggle and steer us toward the hard, right path. We need a Counselor. We need the Holy Spirit, who not only gives us the gift of humility but also empowers us to live a life of humility.[42]

4. Jesus sent the Holy Spirit, "the Counselor," to live inside you and guide you (see John 16:7). What is he saying to you today about how he wants to use you to minister his peace to others?

5. As you consider the peace God has given you, who are some people you know with whom the Lord might want you to share his peace? Write a name next to each type of person below. Then write one thing you can do to share God's peace with each one.

Type of person	Name of person	How you can share God's peace
Family member		
Neighbor		
Someone at church		
Coworker		
Friend		

PRAY | End your time in prayer. Ask God to help you depend on the Holy Spirit to fill you with his peace and make you a conduit of that peace to others.

CONNECT & DISCUSS

Take today to connect with a group member and talk about some of the insights from this session. Use any of the prompts below to help guide your discussion.

What is one new thing you learned about God's view of those who are weak?

How does knowing that God uses those with a humble heart encourage you?

How does it comfort you to know that God knows your name?

Who has been a conduit of peace to you? What have you learned from that person?

What does it mean to walk by the Spirit? How will you seek to do this more?

CATCH UP & READ AHEAD

Use this time to go back and complete any of the study and reflection questions from previous days that you weren't able to finish. Make a note below of any questions you've had and reflect on any growth or personal insights you've gained.

Read chapters 13–15 in *The Hidden Peace* before the next group session. Use the space below to make note of anything that stands out to you or encourages you.

WEEK 6

BEFORE GROUP MEETING	Read chapters 13–15 in *The Hidden Peace* Read the Welcome section (page 102)
GROUP MEETING	Discuss the Connect questions Watch the video teaching for session 6 Discuss the questions that follow as a group Do the closing exercise and pray (pages 102–106)
STUDY 1	Complete the personal study (pages 109–111)
STUDY 2	Complete the personal study (pages 112–114)
STUDY 3	Complete the personal study (pages 115–117)
CONNECT & DISCUSS	Connect with someone in your group (page 118)
WRAP IT UP	Complete any unfinished personal studies (page 119) Connect with your group about the next study that you want to go through together

GETTING OUT OF THE CYCLE

He called out to the LORD, "Lord GOD, please remember me. Strengthen me, God, just once more."

JUDGES 16:28

WELCOME | READ ON YOUR OWN

We've talked about many enemies of humility in this study: fear, ambition, pain, and insignificance. But the root of all these issues—and the greatest enemy of humility—is pride. We find a vivid example of this in the life of another judge in Israel named Samson.

In the previous session, we saw how Samson's mother demonstrated humility when the Lord told her that she would have a son who would save Israel from yet another cycle of sin. She and her husband then showed humility by raising their son in the way God had instructed. Samson, however, did not stay anchored in the humility modeled in his upbringing.

Samson followed the judges Ibzan, Elon, and Abdon. By the time he arrived on the scene, the Israelites were under oppression by the Philistines. Unfortunately, as Samson's story unfolds, his pride—which often led to anger—continually put him into compromising situations that minimized his effectiveness as a judge. This became a pattern that ruined his life and his relationships. Ultimately, it led to great loss and humiliation for Samson.

The good news, as we will discuss in this final session, is that God ultimately used Samson's humiliation to teach him humility. Thankfully, we don't have to wait until the end of our lives, like Samson did, to learn the benefits of submitting to God. Walking humbly with God doesn't mean that we will never suffer, but it does mean that we will know his peace—and more importantly, that we will know the *God* who gives us peace.

CONNECT | 15 MINUTES

Get things started by discussing one of the following questions:

- What is something that spoke to your heart in last week's personal study that you would like to share with the group?

  — *or* —

- When have you seen pride produce chaos?

WATCH | 20 MINUTES

Now watch the video for this session. Below is an outline of the key points covered during the teaching. Record any key concepts that stand out to you.

OUTLINE

I. Over time, the anchors that hold our lives in place can start to shift.

   A. On a boat, a captain has to keep checking the anchor to make sure the boat doesn't drift. This is because the sand on the seafloor will shift.

   B. In the same way, we need to assess our lives at times to make sure we still have an "anchor" of humility in place and we haven't drifted off course.

   C. Whatever we look to as our anchor will keep us oriented in that place. If our anchor is humility, we will stay in the sphere of humility.

II. Samson was like a superhero—but his exploits were mixed with tragedy.

   A. God had told Samson's mother that he would use him mightily. Samson was to be a Nazirite from birth. As such, was not allowed to cut his hair or drink wine.

   B. Samson performed many fantastic feats during his lifetime.

      1. He killed a lion with his bare hands.

      2. He burned the fields of the Philistines using three hundred foxes.

      3. He killed one thousand Philistines using the jawbone of a donkey.

   C. Yet Samson lacked an anchor to remind him how and why to use his strength.

III. Samson's pride led him into situations that put himself and others in danger.

   A. Samson played games with the Philistines at his wedding. His pride was hurt when the men there found out the answer to his riddle through his wife.

   B. Samson's pride was hurt when his father-in-law gave his bride to his friend. His subsequent actions resulted in the death of his former wife and her father.

   C. Samson's pride led him to reveal the secret of his strength to Delilah. He was humiliated when the Philistines captured him and gouged out his eyes.

IV. Samson learned true humility in the final moments of his life.

   A. The Philistines have a victory celebration and make a spectacle of Samson. His posture in this moment is framed by humility through humiliation.

   B. But Samson's humiliation led to humility. God gave Samson one last victory by restoring his strength so he could collapse the pillars in the temple.

   C. "In those days there was no king in Israel; everyone did whatever seemed right to him" (Judges 17:6). When we recognize Jesus as our king, we root our lives in humility, avoid chaos, and find rest for our souls.

NOTES

DISCUSS | 35 MINUTES

Now discuss what you just watched by answering the following questions.

1. Think about the opening story from this week's teaching about the captain having to continually check and assess the anchor to make sure the boat wasn't drifting. What does this say about the need for us to assess whether our "anchor" of humility is holding in our lives? What should we do if we find we are drifting off course?

2. Ask someone in the group to read aloud Judges 14:5–7. This is the first story in Judges in which the incredible gift of strength that God had given to Samson is revealed. However, as we continue to read his story, we see that gift turned into weakness because he lacked humility. When have you seen pride affect your or someone else's service to God?

3. Have someone now read Judges 15:1–6. How did Samson's injured pride in this story lead to the death of his former wife and father-in-law? What are some ways that you have seen pride damage relationships between brothers and sisters in Christ?

4. Samson ultimately learned humility through humiliation when Delilah tricked him into revealing the secret of his strength and he was captured by the Philistines. How did Samson demonstrate humility before God in his final moments? What did God enable him to do?

5. Invite someone to read Matthew 11:29. The cycle of sin we see in Judges could have been stopped if God's people had just chosen humility. But each judge fell short and was unable to provide lasting peace for God's people. How did Jesus break this cycle? What is the promise we are given in this verse if we choose to humbly make Jesus the king of our lives?

RESPOND | 10 MINUTES

Pride isn't a fun topic to talk about, but it is a real problem that we need to address because it can take any of us out. Pride is sneaky, which is why we have to constantly "assess our anchor" to make sure our hearts are firmly secured in humility as our foundation. Take a few minutes on your own to think about how humility and pride have affected your service to God and your relationships with others. Use the questions below to help guide you in this reflection.

In what would you say is your life more fully anchored—humility or pride? Why do you think this is the case?

How might pride be causing disruption in your service to God or in your relationships with others?

What is God saying to you about how you can stay better anchored in humility?

PRAY | 10 MINUTES

End your time by praying together as a group. As you pray, ask God to give you a humble heart that is firmly anchored in him and to protect you from wandering into pride and chaos. Ask if anyone has prayer requests, and then write down those requests so that you and your fellow group members can continue to pray about them in the coming weeks.

SESSION SIX

PERSONAL STUDY

As you discussed in this week's teaching, Samson had a problem with pride that brought about great chaos in his personal life. Whenever his pride was hurt, he reacted with anger and violence. The reason as to why he did this is clear: he didn't stay anchored in humility to God. In fact, it wasn't until the end of his life that he learned true humility through humiliation at the hands of the Philistines. This week, you will have the opportunity to look at a few verses to see what the Bible says about how we can anchor our lives in humility instead of pride and thus experience the peace that we all long to have. As you work through the exercises, be sure to continue to write down your responses to the questions. If you are reading *The Hidden Peace* alongside this study, first review chapters 13–15 in the book.

CHECK YOUR ANCHOR

According to boating experts, "The most frequent anchor-related incidents occur when the anchor drags and the vessel drifts without holding power, which could lead to collisions, groundings or strandings."[43] We might think that an anchor is immovable. But the reality is that an anchor can land on the sand or catch on a rock that is not attached to the seafloor. When that happens, the anchor will drag and move with the current. So, to keep a boat in place, captains have to periodically check the anchor and, if they find it has moved, reset it.

Our lives need an anchor—a device to hold us fixed in a particular place. If we want peace and all the other good things that come from walking by the Holy Spirit (see Galatians 5:1–26), then we must set our anchor in humility. But this can't just be a one-and-done type of process. If we want to *stay* anchored in humility, we periodically need to check our hearts to make sure the foundation into which we have placed that anchor has not shifted.

Unfortunately, it's all too easy for us to drift into the dangerous waters of pride. The results are disastrous—lack of love, hardness of heart, inability to handle an offense, fractured or unhealthy relationships. If we want to avoid this drift, we need to keep checking and resetting our anchors so that we can stay firmly held in the humility that brings peace.

Samson had been raised as a Nazirite and, as such, had been given a foundation based on what it meant to be humble before God. Yet Samson had also been given great power, and with that tremendous physical strength came tremendous temptations to drift into pride. Throughout Samson's life, whenever his pride was hurt, he lashed out at others and inflicted pain on them. He was continually drawn to deceitful women and gave in to their seductive schemes. In the end, Samson was ruined by his pride. If only he had checked his anchor!

READ | Judges 13:1–5, 24–25; Judges 14:1–11; Romans 12:10–18; John 13:34–35

REFLECT

1. Based on Judges 13:1–5, what was God's purpose for Samson's life? According to verses 24–25, what two things did the Lord do for Samson?

2. Samson's life is a paradox. In spite of his ongoing conflicts, God used him to deliver Israel from the Philistines. For each passage in the chart below, write what Samson did out of self-focus and what God was also doing for his people (some passages will include both).

Passage	Samson's self-focus	God's purpose and will
Judges 14:2–3		
Judges 14:4		
Judges 14:5–6		
Judges 14:7		

3. God may be using you for his service, but is it possible that pride has slipped in and is causing chaos in certain areas or relationships? Explain your response.

If we were to make a guidebook for the entire humble Christian life, Romans 12:10–18 would be a key part of it. . . . Living in harmony (or peace) with others requires us to abstain from pride (which leads to concrete hearts). It requires us to surround ourselves with people who are humble—people who don't think they are wise in their own estimation, who don't think of themselves first and others second, and who fight against the temptation of pride at every turn.[44]

4. What is one statement from Romans 12:10–18 that would have helped Samson? What is one statement in this passage that speaks to you—and why?

The love God had for humanity was expressed by sending his Son to the cross. In turn, this kind of love became the model of love for the church (John 3:16; Romans 5:8; Ephesians 5:1–2). Jesus also commanded his disciples to love one another just as he loved them (John 13:34–35; 15:12), and his love was executed in perfection on the cross. It was there that Jesus spilled his divine blood in order to bring people who were once enemies into a new family. It's completely wild, isn't it? *Enemies joined together by blood.* This is the power of Jesus! It's something only his divine blood can do.[45]

5. In John 13:34–35, Jesus commanded his disciples (which includes you) to love others just as he loved them. If you were to reset your anchor today in the virtue of humility, how would it impact the way that you relate to other people and love them as Jesus does?

PRAY | End your time in prayer. Ask God to reveal if your anchor in life has drifted from a place of humility into a place of pride. Pray that the Lord will help you to stay firmly attached to humility.

PRIDE GOES BEFORE DESTRUCTION

The sad and tragic story of Samson reveals that pride in our lives is a killer. It promises power, but it actually makes us weak. And it doesn't cause the kind of weakness to which God is drawn (humility); rather, it causes the kind of weakness that makes us afraid to stand up to sin.

When Samson married a young Philistine woman, he told a riddle to the guests that no one could solve. After three days, the men came to his new bride and threatened to put her and her family to death if she did not find out the answer. Samson's wife spent the rest of the wedding feast crying and nagging Samson. Finally, he gave in. She promptly told her people, and they correctly guessed the riddle. This caused Samson to fly into a rage and kill thirty Philistine men. Her father then turned around and married his bride off to someone else.

Samson later fell in love with Delilah. The Philistines paid her to deceive Samson into revealing the secret of his great strength. Delilah tried three times to trick him, but each time Samson lied and cast off whatever restraints had been put on him. But the fourth time, despite her past record, he told her the whole truth. Why? "She nagged him day after day and pleaded with him until she wore him out" (Judges 16:16). Samson's compromise cost him dearly. Delilah called the Philistines, who quickly overpowered Samson, put out his eyes, and led him to prison.

Pride makes us self-obsessed, which makes us weak. We then give in to pressure from others instead of drawing firm but loving boundaries against sin. If taken too far, this can swallow us up. We need the courage that humility gives to say no to sin and yes to God's peace.

READ | Judges 14:12–20; Judges 16:1–21; Matthew 4:1–10; Proverbs 16:18–20

REFLECT

1. Samson certainly knew that Delilah was plotting against him. Yet despite the danger, he chose to stay with her, and this led to him ultimately giving in and revealing the secret of his strength. When have you remained in a situation where there was temptation? How have you found it hard to say no to things that were unhealthy due to pressure from others?

> Many of us struggle with boundaries because they always come with a cost, both to us and to others. . . . And this is the rub! We all want boundaries to keep us safe, but we also don't want to hurt others' feelings. We long for peace and stability that we feel deep in our souls, and sometimes we can't tell whether boundaries will truly foster this or just create more strife. Honestly, they truly can create more strife . . . unless you have humility.[46]

2. Check any of the scenarios below that you have experienced. On the lines that follow, write how being pushed into doing things you don't want to do makes you feel, and then write down how you tend to handle it when that happens.

- ❏ Someone constantly wants your time when you need to work.
- ❏ Someone accuses you of being unloving because you don't make that person's responsibilities your own.
- ❏ Someone gets angry at you or cuts you off if you don't meet his or her expectations.
- ❏ Someone pressures you to cheat on a work or school project.
- ❏ Someone challenges you on your stand for biblical truths that are increasingly unacceptable in today's society.
- ❏ Someone pushes you to give financially to a cause you can't support.

3. What connection do you find between Judges 14:17 and Judges 16:16–17? Why do you think it is so hard for us *not* to give in to pressure from others—even when we know that what they are asking isn't best for us (or might even be sinful)?

4. In Matthew 4:1–10, we read that Jesus was led by the Holy Spirit into the wilderness of Judea to be tempted by the devil. How did Jesus respond when Satan pressured him? How does this challenge you to use God's Word when responding to pressure from others?

Where there are humble boundaries, there will be the possibility for enduring peace. Boundaries establish order, and order is necessary to experience peace. Where there is disorder, there will be chaos. This is true emotionally, physically, and spiritually. Humility allows us to lovingly keep boundaries so we can avoid chaos and invite peace.[47]

5. "Pride comes before destruction, and an arrogant spirit before a fall" (Proverbs 16:18), but humility allows us to keep boundaries that invite peace. According to verse 19, what is better than the spoils of pride? How is the concept of humility expressed in verse 20?

PRAY | End your time in prayer. Ask God to give you the humility and courage to withstand the pressure to give in to sin, and thank him that he provides everything you need to do so.

FROM HUMILIATION TO PEACE

The final chapter of Samson's story reveals that his pride cost him his ministry, his eyesight, and his freedom. Yet God still saw him. As Samson stood in the temple of Dagon with his hands on two pillars, he had the faith to pray, "Lord GOD, please remember me. Strengthen me, God, just once more" (Judges 16:28). Samson pushed with all his might, the temple collapsed, and three thousand Philistines were killed. In the last moments of his life, Samson remembered humility.

Throughout the book of Judges, we find that every judge fell short. The Israelites did not view God as their king, everyone just did what they wanted (see Judges 17:6), and so none of the judges could provide the lasting peace the people truly needed. The cycle of sin in the people's lives continued spiraling out of control throughout the Old Testament.

Finally, though, the cycle was stopped. Jesus—God himself in human flesh—did what none the judges of the Old Testament could do. And he does for us what we cannot to do for ourselves. Jesus, the greatest and ultimate judge, exhibited perfect, divine humility, first in the incarnation and then in defeating sin and death on the cross.

As we have noted several times in this study, Jesus invites us to share in his life: "Take my yoke upon you and learn from me, because I am lowly and humble in heart, and you will find rest for your souls" (Matthew 11:29). The question for us today is whether we will take him up on the offer. Will we reject our King or acknowledge our need for him? When we follow the humble way of Jesus, we will find the peace our souls long for—lasting and enduring peace.

READ | Judges 16:22–31; Judges 17:6; Matthew 11:28–30; Joshua 24:14–15

REFLECT

1. How do the words of Judges 16:22–31 tell us that God saw Samson in his state of humiliation and yet still planned to use him to accomplish his purposes against the Philistines?

2. When pride or another sin derails us, we often shrink away from God in guilt. But Samson, in his humiliating situation, had the faith to call one final time on the Lord. How do you sense that God is encouraging you today to come boldly to him and find grace and restoration?

> Humility shifts our perspective from the small world of self to the vast world of God. It opens our eyes to his grandeur and reminds us that nothing we walk through is void of his presence. We become God-focused people instead of self-focused people.[48]

3. How should putting yourself under the rulership of God as King affect the way you live? In what areas of your life might you need to acknowledge Jesus' kingship?

4. We have looked at Matthew 11:28–30 several times in this study. How does it help you to know that Jesus doesn't just ask you to be humble but that he also led the way in humility by laying down his own life for you?

> Keep holding on to this: humility is God's gift to you in every situation. It helps you face your fears. It connects you to the power and peace of God. And it turns your unexplainable suffering into a means of transformation, deepening and strengthening you into maturity, as you trust and depend on him more and more.[49]

5. Joshua challenged the people of Israel, "Whom will you serve? Other gods or the Lord?" (see Joshua 24:15). God asks each of us the same question today: "Whom will you serve? Your personal interests, your family, the culture—or me?" How do you respond?

PRAY | End your time in prayer. Thank God that Jesus is the perfect judge who does for us what we cannot do for ourselves. Ask the Lord to help you humbly acknowledge him as King every day of your life that you might live in his peace.

CONNECT & DISCUSS

Take today to connect with a group member and talk about some of the insights from this session. Use any of the prompts below to help guide your discussion.

What is one new thing you learned this week about the danger of pride?

How could humility help you better navigate relationships with other Christians? With other family members? With the difficult people in your life?

How can humility help you better respond to suffering in your life?

Which of the people you studied most resonates with you—Barak, Deborah, Jael, Gideon, Jephthah, Jephthah's daughter, Samson's mother, or Samson? Why?

What will most change in your life as a result of doing this Bible study?

WRAP IT UP

Use this time to go back and complete any of the study and reflection questions from previous days that you weren't able to finish. Make a note below of any questions you've had and reflect on any growth or personal insights you've gained. Finally, discuss with your group what studies you might want to go through next and when you will plan on meeting together again to study God's Word.

LEADER'S GUIDE

Thank you for your willingness to lead your group through this study! What you have chosen to do is valuable and will make a great difference in the lives of others. The rewards of being a leader are different from those of participating in a group, and we hope that as you lead, you will discover new insights into what it means to be humble and how humility can help bring about God's peace in your life.

Finding Peace Through Humility is a six-session Bible study built around video content and small-group interaction. As the group leader, imagine yourself as the host of a party. Your job is to take care of your guests by managing the details so that when your guests arrive, they can focus on one another and on the interaction around the topic for that session.

Your role as the group leader is not to answer all the questions or reteach the content—the video, book, and study guide will do most of that work. Your job is to guide the experience and cultivate your small group into a connected and engaged community. This will make it a place for members to process, question, and reflect—not necessarily to receive more instruction.

There are several elements in this leader's guide that will help you as you structure your study and reflection time, so be sure to take advantage of each one.

BEFORE YOU BEGIN

Before your first meeting, make sure the group members have a copy of this study guide. Alternately, you can hand out the study guides at your first meeting and give the members some time to look over the material and ask any preliminary questions. Also, make sure that the group members are aware that they have access to the streaming videos at any time by following the instructions provided with this guide. During your first meeting, ask the members to provide their names, phone numbers, and email addresses so that you can keep in touch with them.

Generally, the ideal size for a group is eight to ten people, which will ensure that everyone has enough time to participate in discussions. If you have more people, you might want to break up the main group into smaller subgroups. Encourage those who show up at the first meeting to commit to attending the duration of the study, as this will help the group members get to know one another, create stability for the group, and help you know how best to prepare to lead the participants through the material.

Each of the sessions in *Finding Peace Through Humility* begins with an opening reflection in the Welcome section. The questions that follow in the Connect section serve as an icebreaker to get the group members thinking about the session topic. In the rest of the study, it's generally not a good idea to have everyone answer every question—a free-flowing discussion is more desirable. But with the icebreaker question, you can go around the circle and ask each person to respond. Encourage shy people to share, but don't force them.

At your first meeting, let the group members know that each session also contains a personal study section that they can use to continue to engage with the content until the next meeting. While doing this section is optional, it will help participants cement the concepts presented during the group study time and help them better understand how humility will help them see God, themselves, and others more accurately.

Let them know that if they choose to do so, they can watch the video for the next session by accessing the streaming code provided with this study guide. Invite them to bring any questions and insights to your next meeting, especially if they had a breakthrough moment or didn't understand something.

PREPARATION FOR EACH SESSION

There are a few things that you should do to best prepare for each meeting:

- **Read through the session.** This will help you become more familiar with the content and know how to structure the discussion times.

- **Decide how the videos will be used.** Determine whether you want the members to watch the videos ahead of time (again, via the streaming access code provided with this study guide) or together as a group.

- **Decide which questions you want to discuss.** Based on the length of your group discussions, you may not be able to get through all the questions. So look over the discussion questions provided in each session and mark which ones you definitely want to cover.

- **Be familiar with the questions you want to discuss.** When the group meets, you'll be watching the clock, so make sure you are familiar with the questions you have selected. In this way you will ensure that you have the material more deeply in your mind than your group members.

- **Pray for your group.** Pray for your group members and ask God to lead them as they study his Word and listen to his Spirit.

Keep in mind as you lead the discussion times that in many cases there will be no one "right" answer to the questions. Answers will vary, especially when the group members are being asked to share their personal experiences.

STRUCTURING THE DISCUSSION TIME

You will need to determine with your group how long you want your meetings to last so that you can plan your time accordingly. Suggested times for each section have been provided in this study guide, and if you adhere to these times, your group will meet for ninety minutes. However, many groups like to meet for two hours. If this describes your particular group, you can follow the times listed in the right-hand column of the chart below:

Section	90 Minutes	120 Minutes
CONNECT (discuss one or more of the opening questions for the session)	15 minutes	20 minutes
WATCH (watch the teaching material together and take notes)	20 minutes	20 minutes
DISCUSS (discuss the study questions you selected ahead of time)	35 minutes	50 minutes
RESPOND (write down key takeaways)	10 minutes	15 minutes
PRAY (pray together and dismiss)	10 minutes	15 minutes

As the group leader, it is up to you to keep track of the time and to keep things on schedule. You might want to set a timer for each segment so that both you and the group members know when the time is up. (There are some good phone apps for timers that play a gentle chime or other pleasant sound instead of a disruptive noise.)

Don't be concerned if group members are quiet or slow to share. People are often quiet when they are pulling together their ideas, and this might be a new experience for some of them. Just ask a question, and let it hang in the air until someone shares. You can then say, "Thank you. What about others? What came to you when you watched that portion of the teaching?"

GROUP DYNAMICS

Leading a group through *Finding Peace Through Humility* will prove to be highly rewarding both to you and your group members. But you still may encounter challenges along the way! Discussions can get off track. Group members may not be sensitive to the needs and ideas of others. Some might worry that they will be expected to talk about matters that make them feel awkward. Others may express comments that result in disagreements. To help ease this strain on you and the group, consider the following ground rules:

- When someone raises a question or comment that is off the main topic, suggest you deal with it another time, or, if you feel led to go in that direction, let the group know that you will be spending some time discussing it.

- If someone asks a question that you don't know how to answer, admit it, and move on. At your discretion, feel free to invite group members to comment on questions that call for personal experience.

- If you find that one or two people are dominating the discussion time, direct a few questions to others in the group. Outside the main group time, ask the more dominating members to help you draw out the quieter ones. Work to make them part of the solution instead of part of the problem.

- When a disagreement occurs, encourage the group members to process the matter in love. Encourage those on opposite sides to restate what they heard the other side say about the matter, and then invite each side to evaluate if that perception is accurate. Lead the group in examining other scriptures related to the topic and look for common ground.

When any of these issues arise, encourage your group members to follow these words from Scripture: "Love one another" (John 13:34); "If possible, as far as it depends on you, live at peace with everyone" (Romans 12:18); "Whatever is true . . . honorable . . . just . . . pure . . . lovely . . . if there is anything praiseworthy—dwell on these things" (Philippians 4:8); and, "Everyone should be quick to listen, slow to speak, and slow to anger" (James 1:19). This will make your group time more rewarding and beneficial for everyone who attends.

Thank you again for taking the time to lead your group. You are making a difference in your group members' lives and having an impact on their journey toward a better understanding of how growing in humility will bring about peace with God that will last for eternity.

NOTES

1. According to Exodus 12:37, the number of Israelites who left Egypt during the time of the Exodus was six hundred thousand men plus women and children. However, scholars have noted that population estimates for ancient Palestine do not support an Israelite group of this size. One explanation is that the Hebrew word for "thousand" used Exodus 12:37 (*'elep*) can also refer to a clan or a tribe (see Numbers 10:4; Joshua 22:30). Thus, *'elep* here could refer to a military group or division, in which case the text is stating the Israelites had six hundred military divisions. See Bruce Wells, PhD, *Zondervan Illustrated Bible Backgrounds Commentary: Exodus*, volume 1 (Grand Rapids, MI: Zondervan, 2009), 206.
2. Joel Muddamalle, *The Hidden Peace: Finding True Security, Strength, and Confidence Through Humility* (Nashville: W Publishing, 2024), 5–6.
3. Muddamalle, *The Hidden Peace*, 17–18.
4. Muddamalle, *The Hidden Peace*, 21.
5. Muddamalle, *The Hidden Peace*, 29.
6. Augustine of Hippo, *Letter 118* (AD 410), 3:22, emphasis added.
7. Muddamalle, *The Hidden Peace*, 9–10.
8. Muddamalle, *The Hidden Peace*, 6.
9. Muddamalle, *The Hidden Peace*, 32.
10. Muddamalle, *The Hidden Peace*, 33.
11. Muddamalle, *The Hidden Peace*, 48.
12. J. I. Packer, *Weakness Is the Way: Life with Christ Our Strength* (Wheaton, IL: Crossway, 2013).
13. Muddamalle, *The Hidden Peace*, 41.
14. Daniel I. Block, DPhil, *Zondervan Illustrated Bible Backgrounds Commentary: Judges*, volume 2 (Grand Rapids, MI: Zondervan, 2009), 112, 135; Bruce Wells, PhD, *Zondervan Illustrated Bible Backgrounds Commentary: Exodus,* volume 1 (Grand Rapids, MI: Zondervan, 2009), 214.
15. Muddamalle, *The Hidden Peace*, 55.
16. Muddamalle, *The Hidden Peace*, 56.
17. *Merriam-Webster's Dictionary*, s.v. "ambition," https://www.merriam-webster.com/dictionary/ambition.
18. Jeff Kerr, "Ranking NFL Panic Meters for Week 3," CBS, September 23, 2003, https://www.cbssports.com/nfl/news/ranking-nfl-panic-meters-for-week-3-levels-high-for-bears-justin-fields-and-chargers-brandon-staley/.
19. Muddamalle, *The Hidden Peace*, 69–70.
20. Muddamalle, *The Hidden Peace*, 61.
21. Muddamalle, *The Hidden Peace*, 70.
22. Muddamalle, *The Hidden Peace*, 73.
23. Jonathan Edwards, "Humility," C. S. Lewis Institute, https://www.cslewisinstitute.org/wp-content/uploads/humility.pdf.
24. Muddamalle, *The Hidden Peace*, 84–85.
25. Muddamalle, *The Hidden Peace*, 73.
26. James Strong, *Strong's Exhaustive Concordance of the Bible* (Nashville, TN: Thomas Nelson, 2009), s.v. "Tob" (H2897).
27. Muddamalle, *The Hidden Peace*, 98.
28. Muddamalle, *The Hidden Peace*, 18.
29. *Ellicott's Commentary for English Readers, Judges 11*, Bible Hub, https://biblehub.com/commentaries/ellicott/judges/11.htm.
30. Muddamalle, *The Hidden Peace*, 100.
31. Muddamalle, *The Hidden Peace*, 99.

32. Andrew Murray, *Humility: The Journey Toward Holiness* (Minneapolis, MN: Bethany House, 2001), 17.
33. Muddamalle, *The Hidden Peace*, 118.
34. Muddamalle, *The Hidden Peace*, 111–112.
35. John H. Walton, PhD, *Zondervan Illustrated Bible Backgrounds Commentary: Genesis*, volume 1 (Grand Rapids, MI: Zondervan, 2009), 68.
36. J. I. Packer, Merrill C. Tenney, and William White Jr., *Daily Life in Bible Times* (Nashville, TN: Thomas Nelson Publishers, 1982), 19. Note that while women were responsible for maintaining the household, this role extended into business, economics, and other duties, as described in Proverbs 31:10–31.
37. Muddamalle, *The Hidden Peace*, 129.
38. Muddamalle, *The Hidden Peace*, 132.
39. Muddamalle, *The Hidden Peace*, 140–141.
40. Muddamalle, *The Hidden Peace*, 141.
41. Muddamalle, *The Hidden Peace*, 147.
42. Muddamalle, *The Hidden Peace*, 155.
43. "Do's and Don'ts When Dragging Anchor," Safety4Sea, November 19, 2019, https://safety4sea.com/cm-dos-and-donts-when-dragging-anchor/.
44. Muddamalle, *The Hidden Peace*, 183, 185.
45. Muddamalle, *The Hidden Peace*, 169.
46. Muddamalle, *The Hidden Peace*, 181.
47. Muddamalle, *The Hidden Peace*, 182–183.
48. Muddamalle, *The Hidden Peace*, 199.
49. Muddamalle, *The Hidden Peace*, 208.

ABOUT THE AUTHOR

Joel Muddamalle, holding a PhD in Theology, is the Director of Theology and Research at Proverbs 31 Ministries with Lysa TerKeurst and the theologian in residence for Haven Place Ministries, a ministry of Lysa's that provides personalized theology and therapy retreats and smaller gatherings. He also cohosts the popular podcast *Therapy and Theology* with Lysa and licensed counselor Jim Cress.

Joel serves on the preaching team at Transformation Church in Indian Land, SC, with Pastor Derwin Gray and is a frequent speaker for conferences and events (SheSpeaks, IF:Gathering, THINQ Media's Nxt Gen Summit, Hope Heals Camp). One of his favorite things to do is lead in-depth theology workshops and training seminars for churches (FreshLife, Passion City, Transformation Church).

Joel coauthored *30 Days with Seeing* and has had the honor of working with Christian authors in developing the theological framework of their books through COMPEL consulting.

Based in Charlotte, NC, Joel and his wife enjoy a full house with their four children and two dogs. If he doesn't have a theology book in his hand, you can be sure he's either coaching one of his kids in a sport, doing his best to keep up his hoops game on the basketball court, or getting roped into a reel by his wife (@almostindianwife).